D1242337

New York University
CENTER FOR INTERNATIONAL STUDIES

Studies in Peaceful Change

WHY FEDERATIONS FAIL: An Inquiry into the Requisites for Successful Federalism
Thomas M. Franck, Gisbert H. Franz, Herbert J. Spiro, and Frank N. Trager.
New York: New York University Press, 1968

A FREE TRADE ASSOCIATION
Thomas M. Franck and Edward Weisband.
New York: New York University Press, 1968

LAW, REASON AND JUSTICE: Essays in Legal Philosophy
Graham B. Hughes.
New York: New York University Press, Spring 1969

CZECHOSLOVAKIA: Intervention and Impact
I. William Zartman.
New York: New York University Press, 1970

INTERNATIONAL BUSINESS NEGOTIATIONS: A Study in India
Ashok Kapoor.
New York: New York University Press, 1970

SIERRA LEONE: Experiment in Democracy in an African Nation
Gershon Collier.
New York: New York University Press, 1970

COMPARATIVE CONSTITUTIONAL PROCESS
Thomas M. Franck.
New York: Frederick A. Praeger, Inc., 1968.

THE STRUCTURE OF IMPARTIALITY
Thomas M. Franck.
New York: The Macmillan Company, 1968

AGENTS OF CHANGE: A Close Look at the Peace Corps
David Hapgood and Meridan Bennett.
Boston: Little, Brown and Company, 1968

Microstates and Micronesia

Studies in Peaceful Change

Prepared Under the Auspices of
The Center for International Studies, New York University.

New York: New York University Press
London: University of London Press Ltd.
1970

Microstates and Micronesia

Problems of America's Pacific Islands and Other Minute Territories

by Stanley A. de Smith

Library of Congress Catalog Card Number: 74-92526
SBN: 8147-0118-3
Manufactured in the United States of America

Preface

This is a study of some of the problems of very small territories—ministates, microstates, patternless islands and remnants of empire—in the modern world. I have paid special attention to Micronesia, the United States Trust Territory of the Pacific Islands.

My principal criterion of smallness is population. On pragmatic grounds I deem a territory to be "very small" if it has a population of less than 150,000. Some very small territories are sovereign independent states; others are dependent in varying degrees on existing independent states. My interest lies mainly in territories which are already "political entities" in that they have their own systems of government and administration and are not wholly integrated with (though they may be dependent upon) another political entity.

Problems inherent in the fact of smallness have been aggravated by the present structure of international organization and pressures towards decolonization. The opening chapters indicate the scope of these problems and some possible solutions. A further study of the international issues has recently been published by the United Nations Institute for Training and Research (UNITAR); the reader can consult this study, entitled *Status and Problems of Very Small States and Territories*[1] for a mass of factual information. My own book is critical of attitudes in the United Nations Organization, and also dwells in more detail on the political and constitutional problems of individual small territories, a number of which I have visited.

Much of the material for this book was gathered, and some of the thoughts it embodies were assembled, while I was a Visiting Senior Fellow at New York University Center for International

[1] Unitar Series No. 3, New York, 1969. The study was prepared by Mr. Jacques Rapoport.

Studies. I am particularly indebted to Professor Thomas M. Franck, the Director of the Center, who made it possible for me to carry out the work and offered me every encouragement. I am also indebted to Raj Kumar Gupta and John M. Khaminwa, Junior Fellows who worked with me on this project. They are not responsible for any of the opinions I have expressed, and I know that with some of them they will heartily disagree; but we cooperated closely and amicably. I also appreciate being supplied with normally inaccessible information and other facilities by administrators and legislators in Washington and the small territories I visited.

I am grateful to my wife and Professor D. H. N. Johnson for reading parts of the text; to my son Michael for helping with the cartography; to Mr. John C. Bender for energetic assistance in seeing the book through the press; and to Miss Helen Beven and Mrs. J. H. Phillips for typing the script. I also had the benefit of comments from Mr. John F. McMahon, Fellow of Hertford College, Oxford. Mr. McMahon's untimely death in 1969 was a grievous blow to his friends and to international legal scholarship.

STANLEY A. DE SMITH

Contents

Microstates and Micronesia

CHAPTER 1
Introduction

I

Smallness does not have to be an affliction or even a disadvantage. The jockey, the flyweight boxer and the marathon runner have no reason to envy the weightlifter, the shot-putter and the discus thrower or their inflationary diet of anabolic steroids. If the citizens of Monaco, Liechtenstein and Andorra are oppressed by neurotic feelings of inadequacy, the fact has hitherto been well concealed. Nor does it appear from casual acquaintance that Nauruans, Yapese, Tristan islanders or Sarkees devote much of their time to bewailing their lot as inhabitants of very small and remote islands. And wealthy fugitives from burdensome taxes, chilly climates and metropolitan stresses will often stray far afield in quest of a secluded Eden.

The reasons why extremely small places present peculiarly difficult problems lie mainly in the present structure of organized international society. The attitudes generated within that society inevitably tend to produce reactions and reflections within small territories themselves as they become aware of the attention directed towards them.

In the first place, because international organizations exist, it appears to be and occasionally is disadvantageous not to belong to them. One set of problems, which happens to be quite difficult to answer, is concerned with the relationship between very small states and the United Nations Organization and its multifarious organs.

Second, a substantial majority of those political entities which are both very small and, at present, destitute of the benefits attaching to membership of the United Nations are dependent territories. Since colonialism is deemed to be an unmitigated evil which must be speedily brought to an end, and since few of these small territories show any disposition to merge with their neighbors into larger groupings, a fair amount of desultory attention is paid to such territories by the United Nations. This attention tends to arouse local interest in the prospect of accession to full international personality on a basis of sovereign equality with existing independent states, such as the U.S.A. and the Soviet Union. Success in ousting the colonial power, however, exacerbates the problem of finding appropriate niches for miniscule independent states.

Third, administering or protecting powers are more than likely to take a different view of the proper constitutional destination for very small territories under their wings, particularly where such territories are of potential strategic importance. Needless to say, this type of approach does not commend itself to the majority of members of the Committee of Twenty-Four or the Fourth Committee at the United Nations.

A few years ago an informed critic could write: "Colonialism, at least as it is generally defined in the United Nations as Western rule of non-metropolitan areas, is rapidly being brought to a close." [1] No one who has followed the annual jousting at the United Nations over smaller and smaller dependencies during the last two or three years would be inclined to repeat such an opinion today. Perhaps we are nearing the bottom of the barrel, but what remains may be tenacious and the sound of scraping is noisy.

There are other problems, less directly connected with the organizational structure of international society. What internal governmental structure is most appropriate for a very small community? The obvious answer is that a variety of constitutional and administrative arrangements, as diverse as those adopted in large states and communities, may be appropriate; and if one probes deeply one will discover some highly eccentric systems of government in small places. But the tendency is for politicians in small places to demand constitutional forms and status corresponding to their counterparts among their larger neighbors, in much the same way as the smaller units in a federation will press for the full indicia of equality. This type of demand is not easily resisted, and the result of acceding to it may be the creation of an artificial and expensive replica, less serviceable than a simpler and inexpensive model devised to suit the special conditions and traditions of the territory.

At the same time, there is or has been a very conspicuous tendency for metropolitan countries to offer their smaller dependencies, voluntarily or under pressure, a constitutional framework based on their own experience and preconceptions. This tendency is perhaps more evident among the small possessions of the United States than in other places, and it is far from being an unmixed blessing.

Again, smallness in a world dominated by larger forces presents certain fairly obvious hazards. A small territory, autonomous, favorably located, attracting neither envy nor solicitude, may be more secure and serene than its larger neighbors. But so many small territories lack these advantages. They are vulnerable not only to natural catastrophes and to external economic forces, but to the covetous or paternalistic attentions of larger neighbors or great powers. Usually, though not always, they would prefer to be left alone.

Finally, there is the widespread phenomenon of insular particularism (or self-centeredness) which builds up insupportable stresses within island groups and exacerbates other difficulties.

II

For the purpose of this study, no precise definition of smallness will be adopted, but, as we indicated in the Preface, the principal criterion will be that of population. A territory will be treated as being very small if it has a population under 150,000. Hence Greenland, were it not now an integral part of Denmark, would be regarded as a very small territory. Singapore is small in area, but with a population of approximately two millions its claim to be considered individually in a study such as this is weak. Wealth is not a ground for exclusion or poverty a ground for inclusion: Nauru is in, Pakistan is out.

By the end of 1968 seventeen members of the United Nations had populations of less than a million; four of these (Iceland, Luxemburg, Malta and Cyprus) were in Europe and the others were in the Caribbean, Africa and Asia. All but two of them had acquired their independence in the 1960s. At least six other independent states

(Monaco, Liechtenstein, San Marino and the Holy See [2] in Europe, and Western Samoa and Nauru in the Pacific) had populations of less than 150,000 but were not members of the United Nations. The smallest member of the United Nations was the Maldive Islands, with a population of just over 100,000. One could go on to list seventy or eighty other political entities having populations of under a million and lacking the attributes of independence; most are islands or island groups with populations of under 150,000.[3] Apart from smallness and lack of sovereign status, these entities have two characteristics in common: a link with a sovereign state (which may be partial integration with that state, colonial status, a loose form of association or protection, or a number of other relationships importing a degree of dependence) and geographical separation—in most instances separation by a stretch of salt water—from that state. In most cases they can be conceived of as future candidates for independence.

A related but separate problem, which cannot be quantified, is the prospect, recently dramatized in Anguilla, that one or more small elements in a political entity may purport to secede from that entity and then claim international recognition. This type of problem may raise issues both unpredictable and intractable; these difficulties are nevertheless likely to be less acute than when the would-be secessionists are numerous, as in Biafra and Katanga. But because so many political entities, especially island groups, are essentially artificial, the problem is one on which we shall need to dwell.

NOTES

1. Harold Karan Jacobson, "The United Nations and Colonialism: A Tentative Appraisal," 16, *International Organization* (Winter 1962), 37.

2. Whether the Holy See and the Vatican City are separate political entities, and, if so, which of them is a sovereign state, is a controversial problem. One view (see Josef L. Kunz, "The Status of the Holy See in International Law," *American Journal of International Law,* 46 (1952), 303–14, is that the Vatican City is a vassal state of the Holy See.

3. See Tables Ia, II, VII, in the Unitar study (Preface, note 1, *ante*).

CHAPTER 2

Small States and International Society

> A little one shall become a thousand, and a small one a strong nation: I the Lord will hasten it.
>
> (Isaiah, lx, 22)

I

Immediately before the French Revolution, Europe swarmed with diminutive states; most of them were loosely associated within the Holy Roman Empire; some, especially in Italy, had made imperishable contributions to civilization. In the mid-nineteenth century, nationalism burgeoned in Germany and Italy, and by the 1870s the small state had come to be regarded as an anomaly. Under the Versailles Settlement after the First World War, several relatively small new states were to arise from the Hapsburg and Tsarist empires; but, weak or unstable though most of them were in comparison to their powerful neighbors, they were giants when measured against the dwarfs of international society.

The latter half of the nineteenth century was also the age of colonial expansion. Particularly in Africa and in the Pacific, tribal kingdoms and groups of islands were annexed by or (voluntarily or otherwise) placed under the protection of the major powers. Many of the entities whose autonomy was thus extinguished would have qualified today for classification as independent ministates. But at that time it was inconceivable that these "barbarous territories" would take their place as true subjects of international law. Their reemergence, often as artificial aggregates fashioned by the former colonial power, in the guise of sovereign and not so small states, has been the most striking development in the international affairs of the past decade.

II

When the League of Nations was established there were few candidates for membership outside Europe and the non-European areas of white settlement. From black Africa south of the Sahara only two members, Ethiopia and Liberia, could be recruited. Since 1958 they have been joined in the United Nations Organization by twenty-eight black states from the same area.

Among the first members of the League of Nations were not only the British Dominions (which were still "colonies" in British constitutional law, lacking the full attributes of independent statehood for several years afterwards) but also India, which was not even accorded Dominion status during the existence of the League. In these circumstances it is perhaps surprising that the credentials of small but apparently independent applicants for membership were subjected to close scrutiny. But scrutinized they were: the application of Liechtenstein was rejected on the ground that it was not in a position to discharge its international obligations under the Covenant. That Liechtenstein was extremely small (even today its population is barely 20,000), that it had no army, and had voluntarily entrusted to other powers the control of customs, postal, telegraphic and telephonic communications and the normal conduct of its foreign relations, militated against acceptance. Thereupon Monaco, whose foreign relations were conducted under a treaty arrangement with France, discreetly withdrew its application, and San Marino's preliminary inquiries abruptly terminated.

Yet each of these states could reasonably claim to be independent for the purposes of international law. Indeed, Liechtenstein's claim must be regarded as having been authoritatively established in the course of a judgment of the International Court of Justice in a case to which it was a party.[1] Each of them occupies a defined territory, has a regular system of government and participates, albeit to a limited extent, in international relations in its own right. San Marino, a mountainous enclave surrounded by Italy, demonstrated its independence in the most unequivocal form in September 1944 by declaring war against Germany, contrary to the wishes of the Italian Government.[2] Whether Monaco is truly independent is perhaps arguable, for the treaty regulating the principality's relations with France provides that every treaty made by Monaco requires the prior consent of the French Government. Such a limitation on external sovereignty is more explicit than that exercised by the Soviet Union over its satellites, yet it is not necessarily incompatible with Monaco's independence. In marginal cases there is no infallible criterion for determining whether a country is a sovereign independent state. If recognition by other independent states and participation in international affairs are considered major factors, then Monaco can be classified as an independent state. Liechtenstein is admittedly a clearer case: in foreign affairs Switzerland merely acts as its agent, in much the same way that New Zealand acts as Western Samoa's delegate.[3] Cyprus is an acknowledged independent state, though it is precluded from entering into union with Greece, and prescribed foreign powers enjoy by treaty the right to intervene in its internal affairs if fundamental breaches of the constitution under which the Republic was established occur. From these examples we might conclude that a country without power to act in its own right in foreign relations cannot be recognized as formally independent. However, there will be a penumbra of doubt surrounding the status of countries whose competence in external affairs is shared with another state.

Although miniscule states did not become members of the League, they were not wholly excluded from participation in its activities. For example, they took part in conferences organized by the League, and some became members of technical bodies constituted under its auspices. But the somewhat churlish treatment meted out to them by the members of the principal international club appeared to cause little pain and less anxiety; the problem, after all, was a small one.

III

Among the original members of the United Nations were India (which did not become an independent state until 1947) the Philippines (independent in 1946) and Byelorussia and the Ukraine, whose pretensions to independence are unworthy of consideration. Nevertheless, the Charter (Art. 2[1]) provides that the Organization be based on the sovereign equality of all its members. Article 4, dealing with subsequent applications for membership, declares that membership is open to "all other peace-loving states which accept the obligations contained in the Charter and, in the judgment of the Organization, are able and willing to carry out these obligations." The admission of a new member is to be determined by the General Assembly on the recommendation of the Security Council.

Close analysis of Article 4 would be unrewarding. Political considerations usually govern refusal of an application for membership. But it can be assumed that no country will now be admitted unless it first possesses attributes of independent statehood and appears potentially capable of maintaining a permanent mission in New York and paying its share (fixed by the General Assembly as a minimum of 0.04% of the total) of the Organization's annual budget. No application has yet been refused on the latter ground, but the possibility has perhaps deterred miniscule states from submitting applications.

There are, of course, other disincentives for small potential applicants. Not all states wish to cut a dash on the international political scene; some prefer to limit their participation to those matters of special interest to themselves. The cost of maintaining a permanent United Nations mission, though not necessarily prohibitive, is high, as the Maldive Islands confirmed by locating their small mission in the former Maldive Islands Stamp Shop in Manhattan.

None of the European ministates (Liechtenstein, Monaco, San Marino and the Holy See) has in fact applied for membership in the United Nations. Nor has Western Samoa (independent in 1962; population about 140,000) or Nauru (independent in 1968; population 6,000). It does not follow, however, that these states languish in the dismal shades of outer darkness.

In the first place, two of these states, Liechtenstein and Monaco, have become parties to the Statute of the International Court of Justice, although only "states" are entitled to be parties thereto (Statute, Arts. 34, 35). Some may think it incongruous that Liechtenstein's application encountered opposition from Byelorussia on the ground that the applicant was not truly independent. Byelorussia is a wholly integral part of the Soviet Union.

Second, states which are not members of the United Nations may be admitted to full membership of the various specialized agencies.[4] For instance, Monaco and Western Samoa belong to the World

Health Organization; Monaco and the Holy See belong to the International Atomic Energy Authority.

Third, some of these agencies (e.g., the Universal Postal Union) admit to membership territories which have not attained independence; others (e.g., UNESCO) afford associate membership to non-self-governing territories; others provide for the attendance of nonmembers as observers,[5] in some instances with rights to participate actively in the proceedings but without a vote. These diverse practices [6] are not directly germane to problems affecting small independent states in this context. They are, however, indirectly relevant in so far as they may bear upon the future relations between small states and the United Nations Organization itself.

Fourth, states which are not members of the United Nations may be admitted to participation in the Economic Commissions for Europe, Asia and the Far East, Latin America, and Africa; here again there are provisions for associate membership of non-self-governing territories.

Fifth, it is possible for a nonmember state to maintain a permanent observer mission at United Nations headquarters. Monaco, among other countries, does maintain such a mission. Although such observers are given seats in the public galleries, unrestricted documents and social facilities, they enjoy no formal constitutional recognition and have no right as observers to participate. To this extent their status is inferior to that of observers in some of the specialized agencies.

Finally, the interests of nonmember states are not wholly disregarded by the United Nations Charter. For example, the obligation of members to refrain from the threat or use of force in international relations is not limited to other member states (Art. 2[4]). A nonmember may notify the General Assembly or the Security Council of a dispute with a member to which it is a party (Art. 35[2]). And if such a dispute is considered by the Security Council the nonmember is then entitled to an invitation to participate in the discussion (Art. 32).

IV

On the question of the future role of very small states within the international community, one detects several strands of thought.

In the first place, there is a widespread view that microstates ought not to be encouraged to apply for membership in the United Nations since this would impose excessive strain on their own limited resources as well as on the accommodation and administrative facilities provided by the United Nations. The resources of the Secretariat, already tightly stretched, are not unlimited; the quantity of documentation is colossal, and distribution tardy; the proceedings of the General Assembly and some of its Committees are too often prolix and tedious. The United Nations must reconsider the goal of universal membership in the light of contemporary realities.

The Secretary-General has clearly expressed apprehension lest the natural right to independence be equated with a natural right to full membership in the United Nations. In his Annual Report to the General Assembly in September 1967, U Thant suggested that it might be "opportune for the competent organs to undertake a thorough and comprehensive study of the criteria for membership in the United Nations, with a view to laying down the necessary limitations on full membership. . . ." [7] Provision does exist for a special committee of the Security Council to scrutinize applications for membership; but random attempts to bestir it into activity have been fruitless though from time to time various states, including the United States of America,[8] have expressed concern at the admission of very small or impoverished applicants. The problem is latent rather than patent: the formulation of generally acceptable criteria would be difficult, especially as the Maldive Islands are already a member; if criteria were established, their application for the purpose of excluding a recently decolonized state would cause too much embarrassment; and the task would entail hard labor and scant reward. A dearth of enthusiasm for belling the cat is, therefore, likely to continue.

Second, there is, at the same time, an uneasy feeling that the United Nations ought somehow to offer more to new and potential microstates. Thus, U Thant, in the same Annual Report, spoke of the need for devising alternative forms of association with the United Nations' activities, and in particular the formal recognition and definition of observer status.[9]

At present there is no reason to suppose that small nonmember states are more insecure than small member states merely because they do not belong to the United Nations Organization. Nor do they necessarily suffer economic disadvantages; they save money by not having to pay membership dues or maintain expensive delegations, and if they belong to a specialized agency or an economic commission they are eligible for a share in development aid and technical assistance. A recent study revealed that small territories were receiving from the United Nations eleven or twelve times more development aid and technical assistance *per capita* than larger countries.[10] If, like Monaco and the Holy See, a ministate has the means and inclination to establish a permanent observer mission in New York or Geneva, it will have access to a great deal of political and other factual information. There is nothing to prevent an individual observer from ingratiating himself, to his country's advantage, with delegates from neighboring or influential states.

What more, then, is required? Three main suggestions have been offered: a more exalted status in relation to the Organization, an opportunity or right to participate more actively in its proceedings, and a special branch or unit of the Secretariat to deal with the problems besetting small entities. For every solution there are difficulties. Doubtless an attempt could be made to procure an amendment of the Charter to convert informal observer status into a kind of associate membership, with rights to accommodation, rights to speak (perhaps only with leave) in the General Assembly and its committees, even rights to be elected to special committees, but without a right to vote. Whether the prospect of second-class membership in the top international club would prove attractive is questionable. A few ministates might opt for it, particularly if membership dues were reduced or waived for their benefit. But the efficiency of the Organization might be further impaired, were this "second-class" status to prove popular. The creation of a special section within the Secretariat to deal only with the provision of information and technical assistance to very small nonmember states which have no permanent observers is not easily justified at the moment except as a gesture of good will, because the dimensions of the problem are so small. If, however, the problem grows, or if the functions of such a department are to extend to small territories not yet independent, other considerations will arise.

Other suggestions for coping with the problem include representation by a member state, joint representation and limited participation. New Zealand speaks for Western Samoa, and on at least one occasion has been obliged to use two discordant voices, its own and Western Samoa's. Obviously this type of arrangement is possible only where the nonmember has the closest confidence in its member agent. One can also imagine, with difficulty, circumstances where two or more states would agree to being represented by one or more of their number. A more likely contingency is an *ad hoc* cooperative arrangement, such as that entered into by the West African neighbors, Senegal and Gambia, under which Gambia does not maintain a separate permanent mission to the United Nations but economizes by having its representatives attached to the Senegalese mission. Again, the idea that a member might be admitted subject to limited rights of participation, in terms of duration of membership or the scope of permissible activities, has limited attractions and raises obvious problems of definition. But even this idea ought not to be derided. In November 1968 Nauru was admitted to "special membership" of the (formerly British) Commonwealth, with a right to take part in all the Commonwealth's functional activities but not in meetings of Commonwealth Heads of Government. One cannot assume that an analogous arrangement with the United Nations would be unacceptable in principle to the Nauruans.[11]

A more recent line of thought tends to focus rather on what the United Nations might do for very small territories which are not yet independent. To the extent that this might deter such territories from continued political and economic reliance on the imperial power, it can be expected to be well received at the United Nations. The preservation of constitutional links with a weak dependency is popular among administering powers and correspondingly unpopular among a substantial majority of members of the United Nations. Can the United Nations evolve some methods of expediting full decolonization without subsequently becoming deluged with unwanted ministate members and the associated financial burdens? Any idea that the United Nations unfurl a new political umbrella raises the question: who would cluster under it? It is difficult to imagine any existing independent state voluntarily surrendering its sovereignty for such a purpose. Moreover, the association of a dependent territory with the United Nations would be a form of international trusteeship, an institutional device viable only in certain peculiar circumstances. The administering authority as well as the emergent territory would have to agree to the arrangement; and it would not agree unless it could be persuaded that the arrangement might be to its own advantage and would not be tantamount to placing the territory under the tutelage of a body influenced by the prevailing ethos of the Committee of Twenty-Four. Furthermore, it is improbable that any strong body of opinion at the United Nations would favor international trusteeship. And the United Nations Organization is simply not equipped to perform such a task.

Objections would be less strong, on the other hand, if the idea were merely that the new United Nations' initiative should be limited to providing factual information, offering specialized advice and facilitating technical assistance, on a not too preferential basis, for the benefit of very small territories. The United Nations Organization would not be assuming a fundamentally new role. The administrative complications might be supportable and the cost not inordinate. Such a service would also be helpful to some of the existing independent nonmember states, and might dissuade a few prospective applicants for membership from straining their resources. But if, as one must assume, a primary object of the exercise would be to lure the victims of colonialism away from continued association with the administering powers, a measure of cooperation from those powers would still be needed. Would the United States, for example, be prepared to accept a scheme under which the inhabitants of Micronesia, the Virgin Islands, Guam and American Samoa would be directly supplied with material by a special unit of the United Nations, material which would probably underline the virtues of sovereign independence unaccompanied by the burdens of United Nations membership? Would it welcome an incursion of alien experts from unfriendly countries into its territories as a result of a new relationship between those territories and the United Nations? One's tentative answer is negative. Realistic thinking suggests that a new United Nations service along these lines might be most productive in a few cases—British Honduras (Belize) might be an example—where a small dependent territory is on the verge of determining its ultimate status and the metropolitan power is not particularly anxious to maintain a constitutional link with that territory.[12]

Finally, there is the radical suggestion, proposed by Professor Roger Fisher of Harvard Law School,[13] that a new United Nations service, along the lines indicated in the last paragraph, should be made available to small territories which have purported to secede.

No matter how attractively this suggestion may be presented or how attractive may be the secessionists, one is left with the impression that this is a far-fetched invention designed to bring the special case of Anguilla within an acceptable general framework. The objections are obvious: it entails the recognition of the unrecognized, and, more important, it offers the strongest encouragement to would-be secessionists in territories already prone to fragmentation. One can view with sympathy the claim of Anguilla, one can disclaim the notion that Anguilla must for all time be bound to St. Kitts, without deserting the ranks of Tuscany altogether. Claims by small peoples to autonomy and self-determination present massive problems the world over. A grand design which, if implemented, will certainly have the effect of aggravating other individual problems, cannot be accepted.

V

In this short survey I can reasonably be accused of adopting a negative rather than a positive approach. This is partly because my own inclination is towards scepticism rather than dogmatism, partly because there cannot be an all-inclusive international solution to the problem of very small territories, and partly because I do not believe that the problems, considered as an aspect of international organization, are as yet particularly important or urgent. There is no immediate prospect of a flood of indigent applicants for United Nations membership; nor would the admission of a few more small and poor members be a disaster in the eyes of existing members. But the unexpected often happens. If, for instance, the six small states now freely associated with the United Kingdom in the Eastern Caribbean were simultaneously to opt for sovereign independence, then a potentially critical situation would arise, because collapse of this concept of association would have widespread repercussions. One would hope that, in such a situation, United Nations contingency planning might have developed a range of possible solutions adequate to meet the challenge of international relationships in flux. The needs and desires of very small independent states will be diverse, and it should be possible to accommodate them by flexible adjustments to the conditions of membership of and access to the United Nations and its agencics. An advisory clearing-house within the Secretariat, to ease the burdens of very small states which do not wish to become full members of the United Nations or are unable to maintain permanent missions in New York, can be established without any constitutional change. Whether it is feasible for the United Nations to play a really constructive role in dealing with the problems of those very small territories which are unable or disinclined to attain independence is open to serious question.

NOTES

1. *Liechtenstein* v. *Guatemala* (the *Nottebohm* case) (*Second Phase*) (1955), I.C.J. Reports 4.

2. C. d'Olivier Farran, "The Position of Diminutive States in International Law," *Internationalrechtliche und Staatsrechtliche Abhandlungen* (Dusseldorf, 1960), 131, 143.

3. Treaty of Friendship, New Zealand Treaty Series 1962, No. 5. This treaty explicitly recognizes Western Samoa's right to formulate its own foreign policy, emphasizes that New Zealand will act on Western Samoa's behalf when *requested* to do so, and provides for the manner of terminating the agreement.

4. See Patricia Wohlgemuth Blair, *The Ministate Dilemma,* Occasional Paper No. 6, Carnegie Endowment for International Peace (October 1967).

5. On observer status, see A. Glenn Mower, *International Organization,* 20 (1966), 266–283.

6. See, for an exhaustive analysis, *Status and Problems of Very Small States and Territories* (New York: Unitar Series No. 3), 121–156.

7. General Assembly, Official Records, Document A/6701/Add.1, para. 165.

8. See United Nations Document S/8296 (December 13, 1967).

9. *Ibid.,* note 7, *ante.,* paras. 166–168. This was not the first time that the Secretary-General had advanced such suggestions.

10. *Status and Problems of Very Small States and Territories* (*ante*), 196–197. For this purpose small territories were defined as those with a population below one million.

11. Since the Commonwealth has no formal body of rules relating to membership and its incidents, this new development could be introduced informally. Similar changes in United Nations membership would call for amendments to the constituent instruments of the United Nations and its agencies.

12. See *Status and Problems of Very Small States and Territories* (Unitar Series No. 3, 1969), 199–205, for an elaboration of the functions that might be vested in a new United Nations advisory unit.

13. See "The Role of Microstates in International Affairs," *Proceedings of the American Society of International Law* (1968), 164–170.

CHAPTER 3

The United Nations and Dependent Territories: Background and Early Days

> The day of small nations has long passed away. The day of Empires has come.
>
> (Joseph Chamberlain, 1904)

> What can words like "independence" or "sovereignty" mean for a state of only six millions?
>
> (Adolf Hitler, 1938, on Austria)

> The dwarf sees farther than the giant, when he has the giant's shoulder to mount on.
>
> (S. T. Coleridge)

> He that contemneth small things shall fall by little and little.
>
> (Ecclesiasticus, xix, 1)

I

International involvement in the positive advancement of colonial peoples began tentatively with the adoption of Article 22 of the League of Nations Covenant. A system of mandates was introduced for non-European territories detached from the defeated German and Turkish Empires. If founding fathers can be singled out from a congeries of putative parents, one may point to Woodrow Wilson and Smuts. It was Wilson who insisted on the principle of no annexation by the victorious allied powers. It was Smuts who presented to the Peace Conference the concept of mandates (though African territories were excluded from his original scheme) and who later introduced and procured the adoption of the final compromise.

The historical importance of Article 22 was that it embodied the principle of international accountability. Its wording, when contrasted with that of more recent international manifestoes on dependent territories, seems archaic, even mildly comical. To those ex-enemy territories, "inhabited by peoples not yet able to stand by themselves under the strenuous conditions of the modern world," there was to be applied the principle that the well-being and development of the people formed "a sacred trust of civilization." Accordingly, their "tutelage" was to be "entrusted to advanced nations" who could best undertake this responsibility. The major powers would act as mandatories on behalf of the League. The territories concerned were divided into three groups. First, there were territories in the Middle East, formerly belonging to the Turkish Empire. The goal for these territories was independence after a suitable period of protection, to be terminated once they could "stand alone." They were classified as "A" Mandates. The mandatory powers were Britain and France. By 1948 all the "A" Mandates had become independent, and all of them, Iraq, Syria, Lebanon, Israel (formerly Palestine), and Jordan (formerly Transjordan), are members of the United Nations.

Then there were African territories for the administration of which the Mandatory would be responsible, subject to guarantees of freedom of conscience; prohibition of the slave trade, the traffic in arms and liquor, the use of the territories for military purposes and (above all) arming the natives; and an open door policy on trade and commerce. They became "B" Mandates. In practice these territories, Tanganyika, Togoland, the Cameroons and Ruanda-Urundi, were administered by Britain, France and Belgium, the mandatory powers, substantially as if they were colonial dependencies and in some cases as if they were integral parts of existing dependencies. Between 1957 and 1962 all these territories acceded to independence.

Finally, there were Southwest Africa and the German possessions in the Pacific, New Guinea, Western Samoa, Nauru, and the Caroline, Mariana and Marshall Islands. These became "C" Mandates, which could be administered as integral to the mandatory power, subject to similar safeguards as those applicable to "B" Mandates. In fact the individual "C" Mandates did not offer an open door to international commerce. It was and remains convenient for South Africa, in substance though not in form, to appropriate contiguous Southwest Africa by excluding all hostile intruders and imposing its own racial policies on the hapless inhabitants. Although the vestigial mandate survived the League of Nations, in 1966 the United Nations purported to deprive South Africa of it.[1] Now it goes through the motions of administering Namibia by long-range directive and invective through a specially elected council of member-states.

The other "C" Mandates all became trust territories after 1945. The framers of the Covenant of the League had perhaps been unwittingly prophetic in placing the "C" Mandates in a separate category. By 1967 only Western Samoa, under the aegis of New Zealand, had emerged as an independent state. Nauru achieved independence in January 1968. But Australia's other trust territory, New Guinea, and the former Japanese mandated territory of the Pacific Islands (which had come under American trusteeship after the Second World War) remained in a state of conspicuous dependence.

The supervisory functions of the League were exercised by the Permanent Mandates Commission. Four of its members were to be appointed by the Council of the League from nationals of the mandatory powers, and the others—the number varied from five to seven—from nonmandatory powers. They could not be government officials or representatives, but were chosen rather on the basis of individual merit, without a fixed term of office. Nearly all its sessions were held in private, and its reports attracted little publicity. It carried out its functions conscientiously, but its sources of information were derived predominantly from the administering member; visiting missions were never sent to a mandated territory; petitioners were not heard. Because of its sedentary nature the Permanent Mandates Commission found itself at a disadvantage in its attempt to confirm the rumored Japanese violations of Article 22 of the League of Nations Covenant, which outlawed using mandates for strategic purposes. Moreover, the commission, a nonpolitical body, could only offer advice, to which influential members of the League, as well as the United States, chose to turn a deaf ear.

The mandates system had nothing to offer the peoples of the dependent territories. The only reference to them in the Covenant appeared in Article 23, under which the members of the League undertook "to secure just treatment of the native inhabitants of territories under their control." Variously described as "dead wood" and "a functionless appendix," [2] this unenforced obligation nevertheless served as a useful precedent for the more radical proposals made toward the end of the Second World War.

At the outbreak of the Second World War one third of the world and one third of its population were under colonial rule. In India and other parts of Asia, nationalist agitation had attracted the sympathy of Western liberals, and disquiet over conditions in the Caribbean was growing. But most of Africa and the Pacific islands appeared somnolent. It was not only Churchill, the great Englander (as Amery once called him), who envisioned an empire lasting a thousand years.

By the end of 1941, with the Soviet Union, the United States and Japan in the War, the greater part of Europe lay beneath the most efficient and oppressive form of colonial rule ever devised. The war in Europe was already a war of liberation. The nations united in self-defense were deemed to be freedom-loving, and this lent impetus to the aspirations of colonial nationalists for self-government and independence.

The startling Japanese military victories in Southeast Asia shocked countries administering dependencies there. To sections of domestic opinion the weak resistance to the Japanese occupation appeared inexplicable. But with the expulsion of the Japanese, the era of empire soon drew to a close in Asia.

It was impossible, despite the wishes of some of the Allied leaders, to put the clock back to 1939. Indeed, Britain itself had made a post-dated offer of Dominion status to the Indian Congress leaders in 1942. And anticolonial sentiment in the American Government was both vocal and influential.

But the United States Government was obliged to have some regard to the susceptibilities of its allies with imperial possessions. The Atlantic Charter may have proclaimed "the right of all peoples to choose the form of government under which they live," but to Churchill this meant the peoples of Nazi-occupied Europe, not the peoples of the British Empire. Nor were the governments in exile of France and the Netherlands prepared for imperial abdication. And as late as February 1945, Churchill's first reactions to draft proposals for international trusteeship and superintendence over dependent territories were explosive.[3]

Within the United States Government there arose divisions on the future of dependencies. Those responsible for defense matters insisted on the primacy of American strategic interests in the Pacific Islands; international control was all very well, in its proper place.

The provisions of the United Nations Charter relating to dependent territories were agreed to after protracted discussion at the United Nations Conference on International Organization but without acrimonious controversy. Among the founder members of the United Nations, the former recipients of colonial rule were too weak or too closely linked with the United States to carry decisive weight, though their strong views had to be taken into account. The Soviet Union made the appropriate anticolonial noises, but it was more concerned with the urgent problems of securing and extending its frontiers, installing its acolytes in occupied countries, and rehabilitating its own devastated areas; nor was its enthusiasm for colonial liberation (in its modern interpretation) wholly unqualified, as its hankering after a trusteeship over Libya had indicated. Australian zeal for effective international control was tempered by its responsibilities and interests in Papua, New Guinea and Nauru. Concessions were made in all quarters, and the relevant Articles of the Charter were adopted in an atmosphere which, if not quite harmonious, bore little resemblance to the discord so apparent twenty years later.

II

Chapter XII of the Charter (Arts. 75–85) dealt with the International Trusteeship System and Chapter XIII (Arts. 86–91) with the Trusteeship Council. They owed their inspiration to the mandates system of the League of Nations. Chapter XI, ostensibly insignificant in comparison, consists of two Articles, 73 and 74, and is entitled "Declaration Regarding Non-Self-Governing Territories"; it could be regarded as an elaboration of Article 23b of the Covenant of the League of Nations. For trust territories, the United Nations Charter provided supervisory machinery; for other dependent territories, covered by Chapter XI, it provided none. But Chapters XII and XIII are now all but spent; whereas Chapter XI is very much alive, as the remaining administering authorities know only too well.

The main differences between the trusteeship system and the mandates system are the following:

(1) Whereas the League Charter was silent on the political destination of mandated territories, apart from the territories in the Middle East, Article 76b of the Charter explicitly declares that a basic objective of the trusteeship system shall be "to promote the political advancement of the inhabitants of the trust territories, and their progressive development towards self-government or independence as may be appropriate to the particular circumstances of each territory and its peoples and the freely expressed wishes of the peoples concerned, and as may be provided by the terms of each trusteeship agreement."

(2) The trusteeship system was to apply not only to territories then held under mandate and territories newly detached from enemy states but also territories voluntarily placed under the system by administering countries. Only member states themselves were ineligible for submission to trusteeship. The United Nations Organization itself could be a trustee. In practice the former "A" mandated territories, which had or would soon become independent, were not brought under the system. The other former mandated territories, with the exception of Southwest Africa, were placed under the system and under the same administering authorities, save for the former Japanese mandated territory in the Pacific which was transferred to United States administration. Italy, not yet a member of the League, was made administering authority, aided by an international advisory council, for its former colony, Somaliland, for a ten year period terminating in 1960.[4] No other dependent territory was placed under the system. By 1962 Britain, France, Belgium, and Italy had shed their individual responsibilities as trustees. Tanganyika was independent, British Togoland was part of independent Ghana, and the British Cameroons had been divided between the northern part, which opted for integration with independent Nigeria, and the southern part, which opted for integration with the former French Cameroons; French Togoland was independent Togo; Ruanda-Urundi had been divided to become the independent

states of Rwanda and Burundi; Western Samoa also attained independence in 1962. Only three trust territories, Nauru and New Guinea, under Australian administration, and Micronesia, under United States administration, remained in the queue.

(3) Although the threefold classification of mandates was not reproduced under the trusteeship system, one exception to the normal pattern of trust territories was admitted. This was the "strategic area." A strategic area, including part or the whole of a trust territory, could be designated in a trusteeship agreement. The functions of the United Nations relating to such an area were to be exercised by the Security Council instead of by the General Assembly (Articles 82, 83); the administering authority was nevertheless not exempt from the general duty of promoting advancement towards self-government or independence for the people of such an area. The concept of a strategic trusteeship [5] must be regarded as a piece of ad hockery, designed to meet the requirements of the United States. Under the trusteeship agreement concerning the former Japanese mandate, the entire territory now called Micronesia was designated a strategic area. The members of the Security Council unanimously approved the agreement. Unanimity would have been inconceivable ten years later.

(4) Chapter XII of the U.N. Charter, while avoiding the embarrassingly patronizing phraseology of Article 22 of the Covenant of the League, made various references to the role of trust territories and the trusteeship system in the maintenance of international security, quite apart from any designated strategic areas. In particular, Article 84 permitted the raising of volunteer forces and the use of other defense facilities in trust territories. This article aroused a good deal of opposition from anticolonial powers, including the Soviet Union, in 1945. It had no counterpart in the mandates system; today it is anathema.

(5) The machinery for bringing the administering authority to account under the two systems differed both in form and in substance. The Trusteeship Council, unlike the Permanent Mandates Commission, is overtly political. Listed as a principal organ of the United Nations (Charter, Art. 7) under the authority of the General Assembly (Art. 87) (except for strategic areas), it is to consist of three groups of "Members of the United Na-

> tions" (Art. 86): administering authorities, such other permanent members of the Security Council as are not administering authorities, and other members elected by the General Assembly so as to make equal the numbers of administering and nonadministering members on the Trusteeship Council.

The balance was maintained for over twenty years. By February 1968, the Trusteeship Council could no longer be properly constituted in terms of Article 86. For with the independence of Nauru, New Zealand (nominally a joint administering authority over Nauru with Australia and Britain) ceased to be a member, Britain, though retaining its membership, ceased to count as an administering authority, and only two administering authorities, the United States and Australia, were left.[6] It was agreed that Liberia, the only elected member of the Trusteeship Council, should continue for one more year. In 1969 Liberia disappeared, but the Trusteeship Council continued to function. It was then composed of the United States, the Soviet Union, the United Kingdom, France, Nationalist China and Australia.

Although the Trusteeship Council has been a political body, reporting to other political organs of the United Nations (the General Assembly for all trust territories except Micronesia, which, as a strategic area, came under the Security Council), it has proved more objective than its counterparts dealing with other non-self-governing territories. A long account of its activities would be out of place in this study.[7] It has exercised one power denied to the Permanent Mandates Commission—the power to send visiting missions to trust territories. The reports of these missions (from which, however, the Soviet Union has always been excluded) have often stirred the administering authority from complacence or apathy. They have accelerated development in health, educational and economic programs. They have encouraged the mitigation of penal laws and expedited the movement toward self-government. Here one may be making bold assertions on the basis of intangibles. But one can be reasonably certain that the report of the 1954 mission to Tanganyika catalyzed the incipient nationalist movement, to an extent no one would have predicted beforehand: that the report of the 1962 mission to New Guinea ended procrastination and induced the administering authority to establish representative elected institutions; that the triennial United Nations presence in Nauru, coupled with Chief Hammer De Roburt's access to United Nations headquarters, both as a petitioner and special adviser to the Australian delegation, was an important factor in persuading him that Nauru ought to seek independence and in giving him leverage in his political and economic negotiations with the Australian administration; and that the attitude of the United States toward the political future of its Trust Territory, Micronesia, is significantly different from its attitude toward the future of Guam or American Samoa, as a result of the Visiting Missions' work since 1961, and the annual inquisition to which it is subjected at the United Nations.

It is doubtful whether other special features of the trusteeship system—e.g., the admissibility of oral petitions—have been of first-rate importance. Nor has it been particularly important that the Trusteeship Council has been composed of politically appointed representatives of governments rather than a body of "independent experts." A majority of the independent experts on the Permanent Mandates Commission were, in fact, always nationals of the administering powers, mandated or otherwise, and they usually shared the main policy assumptions prevalent in their own countries. The Trusteeship Council has been in a position to ask the administering authority better informed and more penetrating questions—in this sense it has been more "expert" than the Permanent Mandates Commission. As the number of territories under its jurisdiction has dwindled, its expertise has grown. But, with the exception of the Soviet Union and, to a smaller extent in recent years, Liberia, it has not been swayed by the "anticolonialist" ideology which has led its counterparts, in dealing with other dependent territories, to ignore unpalatable facts and to disregard the achievements of the administering powers. Characterized during its first ten years in particular by excessive deference to the administering authorities, its recent record has been praiseworthy in light of the Charter's objectives. But to a clear majority of the members of the United Nations the Trusteeship Council is an anachronism, irrelevant as the guarded phrases of the Charter: it is top-heavy with affluent Western "colonialists"; its investigations lack the ethos of the Inquisition; its field of competence has grown exceedingly small. How much more satisfying life would be if only this council were to be liquidated and superseded by the forward-looking Committee of Twenty-Four!

The Trusteeship Council sometimes found itself in conflict with the organs of the General Assembly in its early years; the story has been well told elsewhere [8] and need not be recapitulated, for its bearing on the main themes of this study is barely peripheral. We can now turn to the penetration of imperial fastnesses outside the trusteeship system.

III

Few could have predicted in 1946 that the mildly worded Chapter XI of the Charter, the Declaration Regarding Non-Self-Governing Territories, would serve as a wedge to be driven into the bodies politic of the administering powers. Article 73, the core of this declaration,[9] may have appeared to be little more than the progeny of the flaccid Article 23 of the League Covenant. It was not adopted under irresistible anticolonialist pressure. Of the fifty-one original members of the United Nations, six were Middle Eastern states, only four (including South Africa) came from Africa, and only three (including India and the Philippines, neither of which was then independent) were indisputably Asian. Five European members had communist governments. Only if one rather unrealistically included all nineteen Latin American members in a national anticolonial bloc could one think in terms of a majority opposed to the administering countries from the outset. Indeed, some of the administering countries themselves—notably Australia, New Zealand and the United States—actively supported the Declaration, and none was willing to demonstrate its lack of enthusiasm by opposing it altogether. After protracted debate, Article 73 emerged [10] as a toothless compromise.

Under Article 73, members administering "territories whose peoples have not yet attained a full measure of self-government" recognized "that the interests of the inhabitants of these territories [were] paramount," and accepted "as a sacred trust" the obligation (a) "to ensure . . . their political . . . advancement," (b) "to develop self-government, to take due account of the political aspirations of the peoples, and to assist them in the development of their free political institutions, according to the particular circumstances of each territory and its peoples and their varying stages of advancement," (c) "to further international peace and security," (d) to promote social and economic welfare and (e) "to transmit regularly to the Secretary-General for information purposes, subject to such limitation as security and constitutional considerations may require, statistical and other information of a technical nature relating to economic, social, and educational conditions" in the territories concerned other than trust territories; the preceding provisions of the Article were *prima facie* as applicable to trust territories as to other dependencies.

Thus administering countries accepted an unenforceable obligation: no machinery outside the trusteeship system had been provided. Article 73 left several questions unanswered. What were meant by such phrases as "non-self-governing territories" and "a full measure of self-government"? Who was to determine their ambit? What was to be done with the information transmitted to the Secretary-General under paragraph (e)? Two points, however, seemed to emerge plainly enough. First, there was no obligation directly cast on the administering authority to submit political information. Second, there was no express mention of "independence" as a political goal, and to this extent Article 73b differed conspicuously from Article 76b, which referred to "self-government or independence" as the ultimate goal or trust territories. But "self-government" was a term broad enough to embrace independence within itself, and a calculated ambiguity was in fact the price paid for general acquiescence in the wording.

In the first instance it was left to the administering countries to decide on the territories for which information might be submitted. The General Assembly appointed an *ad hoc* committee of sixteen members, eight from administering and eight from nonadministering countries, to examine the information, and make recommendations to the General Assembly as to the future procedure. In 1947 it was replaced by a similarly constituted Special Committee on Information, appointed for two years. Its life was extended thereafter for three-year periods. In 1952 it ceased to be "special," but it never became a permanent body and in 1963 its functions were transferred to the more formidable Committee of Twenty-Four.

To offer a full survey of the work of the Committee on Information would be tedious and irksome.[11] Belgium, France and the United Kingdom viewed its activities with misgivings and irritation. Indeed, in 1952 they announced their intention of refusing to take part in its work were it to become permanent.[12] But if the Committee was too radical and intrusive for them, it was too mild and tentative for a growing majority of members of the Fourth (Trusteeship) Committee of the General Assembly which considered its reports. The function of the Committee on Information was never entirely clear. Its powers were limited: it sent no visiting missions, received no petitions, heard no petitioners. From time to time it was assigned special tasks by the General Assembly, such as considering what were significant factors in determining whether a territory was nonself-governing. However, the General Assembly itself tended to bypass the Committee. From 1951 onward, it created a series of *ad hoc* committees to determine the measure of self-government sufficient to absolve the administering authority from further compliance with the obligation to transmit information under Article 73e. In 1953, the General Assembly adopted an amended version of the report of one of these committees, and asserted its own competence, still denied by several of the administering powers, to determine whether the conditions of Article 73e had been complied with in particular instances.[13] It also resolved that questions arising under Chapter XI should be decided by a simple majority instead of by the former two-thirds' majority rule.[14] Pressure, difficult to resist, was exerted on the administering countries to submit political and constitutional information. The United Kingdom was not alone in objecting that such demands, when attributed to legal obligation, amounted to a *de facto* amendment of the Charter,[15] and that the assertion of a general principle of accountability on the part of administering countries to a United Nations organ constituted a breach of Article 2(7), which reserved from the competence of the United Nations power to intervene in matters "essentially within the domestic jurisdiction" of a member state. But by the mid-1950s the concept of domestic jurisdiction, already applied by the majority of member states with a nice selectivity,[16] had become a frail reed for any colonial power to lean upon.

For the purposes of the present study, the following points are of interest:

(1) Long before 1960 a majority of members had ceased to be deterred by the letter of the Charter or its historical antecedents from espousing the general principle that colonial powers were internationally accountable for the administration of all their dependencies.

(2) Nevertheless, no United Nations organ exercised effective inquisitorial functions; and serious scrutiny took place only with

respect to issues that aroused strong emotions (notably Southwest Africa, the Portuguese territories, Cyprus and Algeria) or where the administering power claimed that a listed territory had achieved a full measure of self-government within the meaning of Article 73e.

(3) As we have seen, the original list of seventy-four non-self-governing territories submitted by the administering countries was accepted by the General Assembly. Several points are relevant. (i) The countries submitting information were Australia, Belgium, Denmark, France, the Netherlands, New Zealand, the United Kingdom (with forty-three territories), and the United States (Alaska, Samoa, Guam, Hawaii, Puerto Rico, and the Virgin Islands; and the Panama Canal Zone, till the Panama Government protested that it retained sovereignty over the Zone). (ii) Such countries as the Soviet Union and India (for Sikkim, and the Andaman and Nicobar Islands), which also had dependencies, never submitted information on them and their failure to do so was never successfully impugned. (iii) All the territories for which information was originally submitted were geographically separate from the metropole and most of them were ethnically distinct. Thus, although Australia sent in information about Papua, it never did so for the Northern Territory, which was part of the central land mass though not fully self-governing. Acquiescence in this initial practice shaped the subsequent concept of colonialism. If the United Nations perpetrated a "salt-water fallacy," some of the administering countries were themselves parties to it. (iv) The first returns of some of the administering countries were incomplete. For example, the United Kingdom never submitted information on certain protected states lacking the attributes of full internal self-government. Nor, of course, did it submit information on Southern Rhodesia, because it had internal self-government. Nevertheless, it was later to oppose discussion of developments in Southern Rhodesia on the ground that the affairs of the colony fell within its domestic jurisdiction.

(4) In the early years the Committee of Information did not subject the metropolitan country's refusal to transmit information to very close scrutiny. Thus, the United Kingdom stopped sending information for Malta after the introduction in 1947 of a diarchical constitution conferring a less than complete measure of

internal self-government. In 1949 France secured acquiescence in its decision to send no further information, not only on its overseas departments (French Guiana, Guadeloupe, Martinique and Reunion) which had become at least nominally, integral parts of the metropole, but also on its overseas territories which were neither fully integrated nor fully self-governing.

(5) The most significant contentious issues before the Committee on Information and the Fourth Committee arose during the 1950s. They were concerned with the cessation of information, or proposals to cease transmitting information, with respect to certain listed territories, and with the refusal of Spain and Portugal, after they had joined the United Nations in 1955, to send any information about their overseas provinces on the ground that the territories concerned were integral parts of the metropole. We shall refer to the latter question in the next chapter. The former issue arose in three contexts: [17] the new constitution of the Kingdom of the Netherlands, under which the Dutch Antilles and Surinam were partly integrated with the metropole; [18] the fuller integration of Greenland with Denmark; and Puerto Rico's attainment of Commonwealth status with the United States. The termination of Denmark's obligations under Article 73e in respect of Greenland was approved by a wide margin (forty-five to one, with eleven abstentions).[19]

The Netherlands affair dragged on for four years; finally in 1955 the General Assembly at last accepted by a vote of only twenty-one to ten with no fewer than thirty-three abstentions the arrangements as an act of decolonization.[20] The case of Puerto Rico was disposed of more quickly in 1953, but in the face of still more active opposition; the voting in the General Assembly was twenty-six to sixteen, with eighteen abstentions,[21] though at this date the ideological complection of the General Assembly was not substantially different from that of its original members. But any new arrangement falling short of full integration with an independent state or separate independence for a "colonial" territory, was already viewed with distaste by a growing number of members.

(6) Despite these controversies, and despite the conflicts between the United Nations and several administering powers over claims to supervisory or domestic jurisdiction with respect to the non-

self-governing territories, the General Assembly never posited that every such territory had a natural right to independence. And it did in fact approve as acts of decolonization, constitutional changes falling short of a grant of independence. Indeed, its protracted if intermittent concern with the identification of factors indicative of a full measure of self-government was incompatible with the assertion of any such natural right.

(7) Although the ethos in which colonial issues were discussed at the United Nations from 1960 onward was markedly different from that of the first fifteen years, legacies handed down from the earlier period (e.g., the list of specified non-self-governing territories, the "factors" resolutions tentatively defining the characteristics of dependent status, and the habit of legalistic disputation) continued to have some influence over the subsequent debates.

But let us preserve a sense of proportion. John Strachey's outstanding analytical work, *The End of Empire,* published in 1959, contained not a single reference to the United Nations.

NOTES

1. General Assembly Resolution 2145 (XXI).

2. H. Duncan Hall, *Mandates, Dependencies and Trusteeship* (London: Stevens & Sons, 1948), 224, 226.

3. See Ruth Russell and Jeanette E. Muther, *A History of the United Nations Charter* (Brookings Institution, 1958), 75–91, 540–541. This massive work is the principal secondary source for the *Travaux préparatoires.*

4. Of the other Italian colonial territories, Libya became independent in 1952; and Eritrea became an integral part of Ethiopia.

5. Aptly described as "an excellent example of the subjection of international law to the needs of power politics." D. H. N. Johnson, "Trusteeship in Theory and Practice," 5, *Year Book of World Affairs* (1951), 237.

6. Since the United Kingdom, France, the Soviet Union and Nationalist China, as permanent members of the Security Council, remained on the Trusteeship Council as *ex officio* members, it was impossible to maintain the prescribed balance between administering and nonadministering members.

7. Among general surveys, see Charmian Toussaint, *The Trusteeship System of the United Nations* (London: Stevens & Sons, 1957); George Thullen, *Problems of the Trusteeship System* (Geneva: Droz, 1964). For short but shrewd appraisals, see Inis L.

Claude, Jr., *Swords into Plowshares* (3rd ed.; New York: Random House, 1964), XVI; and Ruth B. Russell, *The United Nations and United States Security Policy* (Washington, D.C.: Brookings Institution, 1968), 30–34, 234–245.

8. See especially Emil Sady in Robert Asher and others, *The United Nations and the General Welfare* (Washington, D.C.: Brookings Institution, 1957), 965–987. Sady's important contribution to this authoritative work, Chapters XIX–XXIII, has also been published separately as a book under the title *The United Nations and Dependent Peoples* (Washington, D.C.: Brookings Institution).

9. Article 74 merely expressed the agreement of the signatories to pursue a policy of good neighborliness in the administration of their dependent territories.

10. See Russell & Muther, *op. cit.,* note 3, *ante.*

11. The fullest account is by Usha Sud, *United Nations and the Non-Self-Governing Territories* (Jullundur and Delhi: University Publishers). See also Sady in Robert E. Asher, *et al., op. cit.,* XXI; more generally Rupert Emerson, "Colonialism, Political Development, and the UN," in *United Nations in the Balance,* ed. Norman J. Padelford & Leland M. Goodrich (New York: Praeger, 1965) 120–139.

12. Belgium did in fact withdraw from participation in 1953.

13. Resolution 742 (VIII); Sady, *op. cit.,* 906.

14. Sady, *op. cit.,* 928–929.

15. The United Kingdom decided to transmit political and constitutional information, but not as a matter of obligation, in 1961. Most of the other administering countries were already doing so.

16. See generally M. S. Rajan, *United Nations and Domestic Jurisdiction* (Bombay: Orient Longmans, 1958); Rosalyn Higgins, *The Development of International Law Through the Organs of the United Nations* (London: Oxford University Press, 1963), Part II.

17. See Sady, *op. cit.,* 908–915, and more fully, Sud, *op. cit.,* note 11, *ante.*

18. The constitution is set out in Document A./AC.35/L.206, Committee on Information from Non-Self-Governing Territories, 1955. The Caribbean territories became internally self-governing. Certain matters of general concern, called Kingdom affairs, are dealt with by joint organs in which the territories are represented. See Sir Harold Mitchell, *Contemporary Politics and Economics in the Caribbean* (Athens: Ohio University Press, 1968), xiii; Kenneth Robinson, "Alternatives to Independence," 4, *Political Studies* (Oxford, 1956), 237–240.

19. Resolution 849 (ix) (1954).

20. Resolution 945 (X) (1955).

21. Resolution 748(VIII)(1953).

CHAPTER 4

The United Nations and Dependent Territories: Slaying the Dragon

Colonialism in all its manifestations is an evil which should speedily be brought to an end.
(Report of the
Bandung Conference, 1955)

And round about the throne were four and twenty seats: and upon the seats I saw four and twenty elders sitting, clothed in white raiment; and they had on their heads crowns of gold.
(Revelations, iv, 4)

I

In 1956, when Japan became the twenty-ninth new member admitted to the United Nations, Asian and Arab representation was becoming significant and the balance was shifting not only away from Europe but also, to a lesser extent, from countries closely aligned with the West. Since Japan's admission, forty-six new members had joined the United Nations down to the end of 1968. Of these new members, thirty-four were African, six Asian, four West Indian and only two (Cyprus and Malta) European. Nearly all of them had acceded to membership upon their emergence to sovereign independence after a period of subordination to a European power.[1] In 1960 alone the African membership leaped by sixteen. It may be mentioned parenthetically that, of the eleven most recent recruits to membership, nine have had a population of less than a million.

Most of the principal colonial empires were already dissolving when the fifteenth session of the General Assembly began in 1960. The British Empire was moving into a state of more or less voluntary liquidation; India, Pakistan, Burma, Ceylon, Ghana, Malaya, Cyprus and Nigeria had become independent. And in his forthright, if slightly naive, "wind of change" speech to the South African Parliament in February 1960, Harold Macmillan had given a clear indication that the rate of decolonization would be quickened. France's political presence was soon to disappear from Africa. So too, less graciously, was that of Belgium. The Netherlands and Denmark had already made their peace with the Committee on Information and the General Assembly. But the scene was now set at the United Nations for the long colonial reckoning.

II

The fifteenth session of the General Assembly had a familiar item on its agenda. Yet another special committee, composed on this occasion of the United States, the United Kingdom, the Netherlands, India, Mexico and Morocco, had been set up in 1959 [2] to study further the principles to guide members in determining whether an obligation existed to transmit information under Article 73e. The report of the subcommittee was discussed at some length by the Fourth Committee but only perfunctorily by the General Assembly. A resolution, 1541(XV), approving the report was passed by sixty-nine to two with twenty-one abstentions. Immediately afterwards the General Assembly passed another resolution [3] calling upon Portugal to fulfill its obligations under the Charter and transmit information with respect to its overseas "provinces." The immediate background was the refusal of Portugal and Spain, after they had been admitted to membership in 1955, to transmit such information on the ground that their overseas territories (e.g., Angola, Mozambique, Timor, Equatorial Guinea) were not colonies or non-self-governing territories, but integral parts of the metropole—an unconvincing assertion. In 1960 Spain succumbed to pressure and undertook to mend its ways; Portugal, to which the overseas provinces were more significant, remained adamant. Resolution 1541(XV), ostensibly an affirmation that the United Nations would be satisfied with a form of decolonization falling short of sovereign independence or full integration with a sovereign state, in fact served as a justification for censuring Portugal. [4] Moreover, it had already been overshadowed by the passing of resolution 1514(XV) (to which we shall return) a few days earlier.

The provisions of Resolution 1541(XV) will nevertheless be summarized. The principles approved by the General Assembly stated that *prima facie* there was an international obligation to transmit information with respect to a territory which had not attained a full measure of self-government and was geographically separate and "distinct ethnically and/or culturally from the country administering it." Such a territory could reach a full measure of self-government in one of three ways: emergence as an independent state, free association with an independent state, or integration with an independent state. Integration would be acceptable only when based on complete equality and equal rights of representation in the organs of central government; and it had to be the result of a freely expressed and fully informed choice through democratic processes (which might be supervised by the United Nations) on the part of the people of the territory concerned. Free association (Principle VII) was not closely defined, but it also had to be the outcome of "a free and voluntary choice by the peoples of the territory concerned through informed and democratic processes." The status had to be one which "respected the individuality and the cultural characteristics of the territory and its peoples," and they had to be free (1) to modify their status by constitutional processes without interference and (2) to determine their own constitution without such interference. If a territory had not achieved a full measure of self-government within the meaning of these principles, the constitutional and security considerations referred to in Article 73e as grounds for restricting the transmission of information under Article 73e were to be invoked only in exceptional circumstances and then only as a limitation on the quantities of information to be transmitted, not as a general exemption from the obligation.

As we shall see, in only one instance, that of the Cook Islands formerly under New Zealand administration, has an administering power succeeded in extricating itself from "the UN hook" since 1960 by means of a free association arrangement with one of its dependencies.

On December 15, 1960, the General Assembly adopted Resolution 1514(XV), the "Declaration on the Granting of Independence to Colonial Countries and Peoples," by eighty-nine votes to nil, with nine abstentions; all but one of the abstainers were administering countries. Almost every development at the United Nations since that time in the field of decolonization has been referable to the terms of this Declaration, the Anti-Colonialist Charter.

It was hastily conceived by a group of forty-three Asian and African members. Its immediate origins were the big influx of newly independent African states and the flamboyant entry, at the head of the Soviet delegation, of Khrushchev, indecorously interrupting a speech by the British Prime Minister to the General Assembly, and calling for the adoption of a resolution demanding an immediate end to colonial rule everywhere. The less immoderate wording of Resolution 1514 was still difficult for the administering authorities to stomach; nevertheless, they found it inexpedient to carry their misgivings to the point of outright opposition.

The Declaration has twelve preambular recitals and seven substantive paragraphs. Declamation and repetition are not absent, but the wording deserves to be analyzed, because of its historical antecedents and the status of the Declaration as a *de facto* amendment of the Charter and as a quasi-theological text.

The recitals refer to the provisions of the Charter relating to fundamental human rights and to the equal rights of nations large and small; the need for creating conditions of stability conducive to the fulfillment of these objectives; the "passionate yearning for freedom in all dependent peoples and the decisive role of such peoples in the attainment of their independence"; the "serious threat to world peace" constituted by the denial of freedom to those peoples; the important role of the United Nations in "assisting the movement for independence"; the fact that "the peoples of the world ardently desire the end of colonialism in all its manifestations"; and the conviction that the continued existence of colonialism militates against the purposes of the United Nations; that the process of liberation is irreversible; that "all peoples have an inalienable right to complete freedom, the exercise of their sovereignty and the integrity of their national territory." Accordingly, the Resolution "solemnly proclaims the necessity of bringing to a speedy and unconditional end colonialism in all its forms and manifestations."

The substantive paragraphs declare that (1) the subjection of peoples to alien domination and exploitation is a denial of human rights, is contrary to the Charter and impedes the promotion of world peace and cooperation; (2) all peoples have the right to self-determination; (3) inadequacy of political, economic, social, or educational preparedness should "never serve as a pretext for delaying independence"; (4) all repressive measures directed against dependent peoples must cease so they can exercise their right to complete independence, "and the integrity of their national territory shall be respected"; (5) immediate steps shall be taken in all territories which have not attained independence, to transfer all powers to the peoples of those territories, so as to enable them to enjoy complete independence; (6) any attempt aimed at the "disruption of the national unity and the territorial integrity of a country" is incompatible with the Charter; (7) all states shall observe the provisions of the Charter, the Universal Declaration of Human Rights and the present Declaration "on the basis of equality, noninterference in the internal affairs of all States, and respect for the sovereign rights of all peoples and their territorial integrity."

A number of comments need to be made.

(1) Only by a very strained interpretation can the Declaration itself be regarded as compatible with the Charter. Chapters XI, XII and XIII of the Charter necessarily presuppose the legitimacy of the administration of non-self-governing territories by other countries. The Declaration, calling for a speedy and unconditional end to "colonialism in all forms and manifestations" (a phrase adapted from the report of the Bandung Conference of nonaligned countries) does not define colonialism; but in asserting that the subjection of peoples to "alien domination" is itself contrary to the Charter and in insisting on the need for taking immediate steps to liquidate the trusteeship system and to liberate non-self-governing territories it gives the clear impression of denying the legitimacy of any colonial-type relationship that the General Assembly might choose to identify.

(2) The Declaration, in the course of standing the chapters of the Charter on their heads, makes oblique but telling references to other provisions of the Charter. Thus, among the proclaimed purposes of the United Nations (Charter, Art. 1) are the maintenance of international peace and security, the development of friendly relations on the basis of respect for the equal rights and self-determi-

nation of peoples, and the encouragement of respect for human rights. The continuance of colonial rule, so the Declaration asserts, frustrates these purposes. Article 55 of the Charter reiterates that the promotion of self-determination and respect for human rights are obligations of the United Nations. Again, Article 2(4) requires members to refrain in international relations from the threat or use of force against the territorial integrity or political independence of any state. The Declaration turns this phrase neatly against the colonial powers.

(3) The domestic jurisdiction clause, Article 2(7), of the Charter is virtually emptied of content in matters involving colonialism. In any event Article 2(7) was already qualified by a reference to enforcement measures required for the purpose of removing threats to peace.

(4) The Declaration affirms that all peoples have an "inalienable" right to complete freedom. The only form of freedom for dependent peoples mentioned in the Declaration is independence; the word "independence" appears eight times. What of Resolution 1541(XV) with its examination of permissible alternatives to independence? What indeed?

(5) Since independence is an inalienable right, a colonial people cannot legitimately elect to remain subject to the yoke of colonialism. This is just as inadmissible as consent by a slave to the perpetuation of his enslavement. For this reason alone, the referendum organized by Britain in Gibraltar in September 1967, in which over 99% of the electorate expressed the wish to remain under British rule rather than be incorporated in Spain, was quite unacceptable.[5]

(6) The Declaration asserts that inadequacy of preparedness should never serve as a "pretext" for delaying independence. The use of the word "pretext" could be understood as implying that, in some situations, acceptable *bona fide* reasons might exist for delaying independence. Because such an interpretation was possible, some members were induced to vote in favor of, or not to oppose, Resolution 1514. But in practice the word "reason" has come to be substituted for "pretext." [6] The fact that a territory is very tiny, isolated and desperately poor is not an acceptable "pretext" for delaying independence.

(7) Although the Declaration links colonialism with racial

discrimination only in a loose way, and mainly through its general references to the denial of human rights, subsequent resolutions of the General Assembly have pulled the two phenomena more closely together. Thus, Resolution 2105(XX)(1965) asserts that "the continuation of colonial rule and the practice of *apartheid* as well as all forms of racial discrimination threaten international peace and security and constitute a crime against humanity."

(8) The ostensibly all-embracing references to the principle of self-determination must be strictly limited to the colonial context. They were not intended to furnish any legitimate foundation for secessionist movements within existing independent states or, for that matter, within dependent territories.

(9) The "self" to be determined is the entire colonial territory. It must not be dismembered by the colonial power, before or at the time of independence. Hence it was reprehensible for the United Kingdom to create a new colony, the British Indian Ocean Territory, in 1965 by detaching remote island groups from Seychelles and Mauritius, particularly as the colonial power envisaged the use of the territory for strategic purposes.[7] Indeed, the United Nations have refused to recognize the existence of this territory. Again, it was wrong for the United Kingdom to retrocede the Kuria Muria islands, which had been administered with the South Arabian Federation, to Muscat and Oman when South Arabia became independent in 1967 as the Peoples' Republic of Southern Yemen. The territorial integrity of the "colonial" entity must not be disrupted.

(10) The frequent references to human rights in the Declaration can be regarded as perfectly sincere, when read in their context. But there is a stark contrast between the solicitude of so many members for this aspect of human rights and their tenacious reliance on the principle of domestic jurisdiction in the face of complaints about denial of fundamental rights in their own political systems. The Human Rights Commission has been perhaps the least effective of all organs of the United Nations, except as a source from which worthy but inoffensive resolutions, covenants and conventions have originated.[8]

(11) Subsequent general resolutions of the Assembly denouncing the use or threat of force in international relations [9] and asserting the right of peoples to permanent sovereignty over their natural

resources [10] were closely linked with Resolution 1514(XV) and the campaign against colonialism and neo-colonialism, though their ambit was also broader.

In the light of these remarks, the treatment of two subsequent issues affecting small territories, Goa and Gibraltar, becomes more comprehensible. In December 1961 Indian troops marched into Goa, a Portuguese enclave in the Indian subcontinent, and the territory was annexed by India. Far from treating this as an act of aggression, a majority of members acclaimed the Indian Government's action. India had implemented Resolution 1514, admittedly by an unorthodox method: the people of Goa had achieved independence (though hardly by an act of self-determination); the threat to peace symbolized by the Portuguese presence had been liquidated; the territorial integrity of India had been restored. Some were willing to characterize colonialism as a form of permanent aggression.[11] Recent resolutions of the General Assembly have called upon all states to render colonial liberation movements moral and material assistance.[12]

In December 1967 the General Assembly passed a resolution [13] which not only condemned the holding of the referendum in Gibraltar by the administering power but invited the Governments of Spain and the United Kingdom to resume negotiations "with a view to putting an end to the colonial situation in Gibraltar" and asserted that "any colonial situation which partially or completely destroys the national unity and territorial integrity of a country" was "incompatible with the purposes and principles of the Charter" and specifically with paragraph 6 of Resolution 1514. In other words, the United Kingdom was violating international law and the territory of Spain by its presence in Gibraltar, and was to hand the Rock back to Spain against the known wishes of a huge majority of its inhabitants. To be fair, one should mention that this resolution was passed by a relatively narrow majority (seventy-three to nineteen with twenty-seven abstentions).[14] Fairness also makes it necessary to mention that Spain, a Fascist country, had a regime no more authoritarian than those of a sizeable majority of United Nations members, was in the process of shedding its last imperial possessions, had been a staunch supporter of the Arab states in their war with Israel, had many friends in Latin America, and was thought to be potentially detachable from its strategic involvement with the United States; [15] and that Britain, a parliamentary social democracy, still not a wholly insignificant imperial power, was saddled with the Rhodesian albatross, maintained a base in Gibraltar and was a close ally of the United States. A more peremptory resolution, calling on Britain to remove itself from Gibraltar by October 1969, was passed in December 1968, but by a slightly smaller majority (sixty-seven to eighteen with thirty-four abstentions).[16]

III

In 1961 the General Assembly set up a special committee of seventeen members, only three of which (the United States, the United Kingdom and Australia) were administering authorities, to study the application of the 1960 Declaration and to report progress. In the same year it established special committees on Southwest Africa and the Portuguese territories, and extended the terms of reference of the Committee on Information to include the study of political information. In 1962 the membership of the Special Committee of Seventeen was enlarged to twenty-four, and it took over the functions then exercised by the special committees on Southwest Africa and the Portuguese territories. The following year the Committee on Information was dissolved and its functions transferred to the Committee of Twenty-Four, officially designated as the "Special Committee on the Situation with regard to the Implementation of the Declaration on the Granting of Independence to Colonial Countries and Peoples." Its terms of reference [17] were wide enough to be construed as embracing the implementation of the Declaration in trust territories. The more spectacular activities of the Committee of Twenty-Four have overshadowed the earnest plodding of the Trusteeship Council.

The Committee has been composed of seven African members, five Asian members, four European Communist members, three Latin American members, one from Northern Europe, one other from Western Europe, the United States, the United Kingdom and Australia.[18] Hence it has a large built-in anticolonial majority. So has the General Assembly. And this majority is still growing as colonies accede to independence and are admitted to membership.

The Committee is kept well supplied by the Secretariat with factual information, much of which emanates from the administering authorities. When it discusses a particular territory, in full Committee or in one of its area subcommittees, the administering authority and any other interested members are invited to attend, make a statement and answer questions. The subcommittee and then the main Committee will prepare reports and resolutions, which will be transmitted to the Fourth Committee for further debate. Debates in the General Assembly on the reports and resolutions seldom go into points of detail except on particularly contentious issues like Rhodesia, the Portuguese territories or Gibraltar. Read with discrimination, these often voluminous proceedings furnish a major source of information on developments in little-known territories.

The Committee also receives written petitions and may even decide to hear a petitioner. It has recently paid annual visits to Africa in order to hear petitioners. Its desire to send visiting missions to spread the light and gather information in dependent territories has been thwarted by the refusal of administering authorities to receive such missions. The Committee may be entrusted by the Assembly with special tasks: e.g., the study of military action by colonial powers, and an investigation of the activities of foreign economic interests in colonial territories, which may be impeding the implementation of Resolution 1514. The Assembly has also instructed it to pay particular attention to the problem of small territories.[19]

The Committee determines which are the territories subject to its jurisdiction. Few changes were made from the list used by the Committee on Information. Some have been deleted as the process of decolonization continues; a small number of additions have been made. Of the French overseas territories, only French Somaliland had been added by 1968; this was at once an indication of the extent to which the Committee is Africa-oriented and of its desire not to give undue offense to President de Gaulle.

This is not the place to attempt a full evaluation of the work of the Committee of Twenty-Four. A few remarks, however, are worth making. In the first place, the Committee does not purport to be a dispassionate commission of inquiry. It is the General Assembly's chosen instrument for procuring the eviction of the administering authorities at the earliest possible moment. Second, it follows from this that it will usually harry, often condemn and seldom offer any suspicion of a compliment to an administering authority; that harsh judgments tend to be warmly acclaimed by a substantial majority of member states; that representatives on the Committee can build up international and domestic reputations by the vehemence of their verbal assaults on colonialism, provided that they preserve the forms of personal decorum; that other representatives on the Committee are reluctant to appear "soft on colonialism" or to prejudice the extraneous interests of their own countries, by publicly opposing the position taken up by a majority or even by a radical minority and that the remaining administering authorities are driven to extremes of exasperation by the criticism their countries incur, the short shrift that is given their own statements and arguments, and the tone and content of the resolutions passed by the Committee (seldom amended by the Fourth Committee or the General Assembly). Third, for its first three years the Committee was concerned, naturally enough, with the problems of southern Africa. Here, save in the former British High Commission territories of Bechuanaland (now Botswana), Basutoland (now Lesotho) and Swaziland, the political difficulties proved quite intractable; colonial rule was based on white minority domination over a colored majority who were subjected to humiliating political and social discrimination. This, surely, was colonialism incarnate and obdurate. And those countries which had allowed this situation to come about or those without the will to end it were blameworthy. In such a context, African countries in particular could readily be persuaded to damn the colonialists and all their works elsewhere. One can sympathize with, even share, an abhorrence of white racial arrogance,[20] without blinding oneself to abhorrent realities in other types of group relationships or adopting a doctrinaire approach to superficially analogous situations. Fourth, when members turned their attention to the Caribbean, the Pacific and the Indian Ocean, they could not be expected to fully appreciate all the local issues. Their repeated insistence on the need to send out visiting missions to non-self-governing territories in these areas has unfortunately been accompanied by a disinclination to accept the truth, whenever facts are discordant with their own preconceptions. That the Committee's would-be emissaries have been unwelcome guests is hardly surprising. Why accept visits from those who claim to know the answer before having acquired a proper command of the facts? Fifth, the Committee's obsession with independence as the answer to colonial problems makes it difficult for some of its demands to be treated seriously. Each year it insists that independence be granted to Pitcairn, an island of fewer than ninety inhabitants.

Nevertheless, the Committee has not been uniformly inflexible in its approach to individual problems. It recognizes that some colonies may best achieve their independence by merger. Where State *A* has claimed sovereignty over territory *B* which is administered as a dependency of State *C,* the Committee has urged *A* and *C* to negotiate, instead of demanding immediate independence for *B;* it has adopted this attitude with regard to the disputes between Britain and Argentina over the Falkland Islands (Islas Malvinas), between Britain and Guatemala over British Honduras (Belize), between Britain and Spain over Gibraltar, and between Morocco and Spain over Ifni (now ceded to Morocco). It modified its position over Gibraltar in 1967 by accepting the Spanish claim to assume sovereignty over the Rock. The Committee will probably modify its position with regard to British Honduras, a strong candidate for independence in the near future.

Again, it has shown some appreciation of the unsatisfactory political fragmentation in the Caribbean, at least in the course of subcommittee proceedings, where some emphasis has been laid on the desirability of forging a new and independent federal grouping, despite the failure of two recent attempts to establish a viable federation of British territories in the region.

And there was the singular case of the Cook Islands. This group of islands in the South Pacific, scattered over 850,000 square miles of ocean with a total land area of some ninety square miles and a population of barely 20,000, became a dependent territory of New Zealand in 1901. New Zealand, the smallest and, by present standards, the most progressive of the "colonial" powers, had actively encouraged the independence movement in its trust territory, Western Samoa—a movement which reached its destination in 1962.[21] The same year, the New Zealand Government took the initiative in suggesting to the Cook Islands Legislative Assembly that four possible alternative constitutional goals should be considered: independence, integration with New Zealand, membership in a (nonexistent) Polynesian federation, or full internal self-government. The Assembly unanimously preferred the last alternative. In 1963 the New Zealand Government sent out a commission of three constitutional experts to advise the Cook Islands Legislative Assembly on the form of the future constitution and its relationships with New Zealand. Their report, accepted by the Assembly, furnished the basis for the Cook Islands Constitution Act in 1964,[22] passed by the New Zealand Parliament after extensive consultations with the Cook Islanders. The new constitutional arrangements were legitimized only after a General Election in the Cook Islands in 1965.

New Zealand kept the United Nations informed of these developments, inviting the Secretary-General to nominate delegates to the Cook Islands to act on behalf of the United Nations during and after the election campaign. A United Nations Supervisor of Elections was appointed—in substance he observed rather than supervised—and reported [23] that the elections, in which the new constitutional scheme was approved, had been free and fair. The scheme was brought into operation in August 1965.

The association scheme gave the Cook Islands complete internal self-government, including full powers of constitutional amendment and power to terminate the relationship with New Zealand unilaterally by following a prescribed constitutional procedure. New Zealand retained responsibility for defense and external affairs, and was represented in the Cook Islands by a High Commissioner, who also exercised functions characteristic of those of a Governor-General, the constitutional representative of the Head of State. The High Commissioner could also exercise minor delaying powers and more important powers of initiative. But the New Zealand Government retained no legal authority, either directly or through the medium of the High Commissioner, to implement its responsibilities for the defense and external affairs of the Islands except at the request of the Cook Islands Government. In short, this was essentially an act of faith on the part of the New Zealand Government—an act no doubt facilitated by the value the Cook Islanders placed on their New Zealand citizenship, their unrestricted freedom to emigrate to New Zealand and the 80% contribution made by New Zealand to the local budget.

If, then, Resolution 1541(XV) still had any meaning at all, the Cook Islands had determined their own future by opting for free association with an independent state, and the former administering power was absolved of its obligations to transmit information under Article 73e of the Charter. The Committee of Twenty-Four, not entirely happy at this outcome, passed a somewhat noncommittal resolution, expressing its appreciation, taking note of what had happened, but omitting any reference to Article 73e. The Italian representative, who wished to amend the motion so as to introduce an explicit reference to New Zealand's fulfillment of its obligation under the Article, observed that the majority of the Committee were not yet "psychologically prepared" for such a step.[24] The Fourth Committee [25] did in fact pass a more satisfactory resolution, but not before an amendment to delete a passage to the effect that the Cook Islanders had assumed control of their future had been defeated by the narrowest possible margin (twenty-nine to twenty-eight with forty-three abstentions). The General Assembly's resolution on the subject [26] accepted the act as one of self-determination, recorded that transmission of information under Article 73e was no longer necessary, but went on to reaffirm the responsibility of the United Nations under Resolution 1514(XV) to assist the Cook Islanders "in the eventual achievement of full independence, if they so wish, at a later date." The right to independence was, after all, inalienable.

The reluctant concession to political reality made by the Fourth Committee, and to a lesser extent by the Committee of Twenty-Four, in the case of the Cook Islands was mildly encouraging. For many tiny island dependencies, poor and remote, the concept of sovereign independence simply did not make sense. For them decolonization by means of a free association with another state, normally the former administering power, would be the most appropriate political solution. But precedent was not to broaden downwards. At the end of 1969 the Cook Islands remained the only nonself-governing territory acknowledged by the United Nations, since the watershed of 1960, to have achieved a full measure of self-government without full independence.

None of the 1965 resolutions on the Cook Islands mentioned the apparently unmentionable Resolution 1541. In 1966 a subcommittee of the Committee of Twenty-Four incautiously referred to Resolution 1541, as well as to Resolution 1514, in the context of the decolonization of the United States Virgin Islands; the full Committee shrewdly excised the reference to Resolution 1541. Meanwhile, the United Kingdom Government, probing for alternatives to independence for its own very small island dependencies, had been attending the course of the Cook Islands experiment and, pinning its hopes to another tacit recognition of the legitimacy of association as a means of decolonization, sought a way out of its difficulties in the Caribbean. These difficulties were formidable. A West Indies Federation, incorporating Jamaica, Trinidad, Barbados and the Leeward and Windward Islands, had been created in 1958. Four years later the federal scheme was in ruins, and on the day the Federation had been destined for independence, it was instead dissolved. Attempts to create a second federation (without Jamaica and Trinidad, which had become independent in 1962) were thwarted;[27] in 1965 they were finally abandoned. Barbados, with a population of a quarter of a million, was to go it alone, and became independent in 1966. But there would remain a number of island colonies in the region. Some had the resources adequate to support the usual attributes of internal self-government; none had a population of over 100,000, or the revenue a country would need to sustain the trappings of full independence, and none appeared anxious to gyrate on the international scene. On the other hand, the United Kingdom was committed to decolonization as rapidly as possible, seeing no reason to present itself any longer as a major target for anticolonialist rancour at the United Nations.

Thus there emerged the British scheme for associated statehood in the eastern Caribbean, applying to the territories of Grenada, St. Lucia, St. Vincent, Dominica, St. Kitts-Nevis-Anguilla, and Antigua. The miniscule territories in the region—Montserrat, the Cayman Islands, and the British Virgin Islands—were not covered by the scheme; nor, for various reasons, were the Bahamas, the Turks and Caicos Islands, Bermuda, or British Honduras. Details of the scheme were announced at the end of 1965; constitutional conferences with elected members of the several legislatures were held in London in 1966, and the main principles were unanimously agreed upon, subject to minor modifications for certain of the territories. Enabling legislation was passed early in 1967. And associated statehood (except for St. Vincent [where a controversial change of government interposed a period of delay lasting until October 1969]) came into effect for all the territories shortly afterwards.[28]

There had been no United Nations involvement in this process of self-determination. Nor had there been any direct United Nations involvement in the processes by which other British dependencies had reached independence, save in the case of trust territories in West Africa and to a small extent in British Guiana and Aden. Except in Anguilla there was no serious opposition to the scheme for associated statehood. Moreover, in all but one of the associated states, elections had been held shortly before statehood. Apart from the exclusion of a

United Nations presence, the only substantial differences between the British Caribbean and the Cook Islands model were (1) that the United Kingdom Government retained executive and legislative powers to effect its responsibilities for defense and external affairs with respect to the associated states, and (2) that it was made easier for an associated state to enter into a federation, union or other form of association with an independent Commonwealth country in the Caribbean than for the state to move unilaterally to full independence.[29] But associated states, like the Cook Islands, were given full powers of constitutional amendment, the right of unilateral secession, and a degree of internal legislative autonomy analogous to that enjoyed by the British dominions after the Statute of Westminster 1931. Moreover, powers were delegated to their governments to conduct external relations in a number of fields; and they have participated in the functional activities of the Commonwealth in much the same way as Nauru, a sovereign state, now participates in them. The degree of autonomy thus conceded was wider than that accorded by the United States to Puerto Rico in 1952, and substantially wider than that enjoyed by the French overseas territories.

However, these were in the mid-1960s. Any arrangement guised as an act of decolonization which left the colonial power with a foot inside the door was to be viewed with profound suspicion. And Britain was in bad odor with African and Asian states over Rhodesia, with the Arab states over attitudes toward Israel, and with Viet Cong sympathizers because of its alliance with the United States. In 1967 the Committee of Twenty-Four decided, by a large majority, not to accept the *fait accompli* in the West Indies as a bona fide act of decolonization.[30] The Fourth Committee and the General Assembly affirmed this decision. Purportedly the main objection to the British-sponsored scheme was procedural rather than substantive.[31] The United Nations had been ignored until the decisions had been made; no pains had been taken to impress upon the islanders the benefits, moral or material, of independence; and although the idea of association was not to be condemned out of hand, the administering power had failed to discharge the onus of proving that this scheme was what the people really wanted.

Britain stopped supplying the United Nations with information on the associated states, although they are still discussed by the Committee of Twenty-Four as if they were colonies: petitions are received, petitioners heard, and the heads of government in the associated states still have no international forum for answering their traducers.

There may be a danger of exaggerating the significance of the United Nations decisions on the question of the Caribbean associated states. Each case, as an English judge might say, must turn on its own particular facts. Perhaps the Caribbean decision ought not to be given greater weight as a precedent than that in the case of the Cook Islands. Certainly any case made by Britain in 1967 was assured of a hostile reception, not only in connection with Rhodesia and Gibraltar but with other colonial matters as well. For example, the proceedings in the Committee of Twenty-Four over the affairs of the colony of Mauritius (which was about to become independent) were enlivened by a number of assertions which, in the writer's personal knowledge, were palpably absurd.[32] But Britain was not the only target. New Zealand, surely the exemplar of a cooperative administering country, was taken severely to task for failing to expedite progress towards independence in its minute, poor and inward-looking dependencies of Niue (population 5,000) and the Tokelau Islands (population 1,800). And the criticisms were renewed with more acerbity in 1968.[33] Again, in 1967 the Committee of Twenty-Four adopted a report[34] on the activities of foreign economic and other interests which were impeding the implementation of Resolution 1514(XV). This report, approved only "in general" by the General Assembly,[35] abounded in demonstrably inaccurate propositions insofar as they were asserted to be of universal application.[36]

These comments, which could be amplified by other illustrations, indicate a marked swing toward fundamentalist and doctrinaire approaches to Resolution 1514 and away from Resolution 1541, toward the idea that independence is the only acceptable solution for a colonial people save in very extraordinary circumstances. If independence is offered, then, save in very extraordinary circumstances, there will be no demand at the United Nations that the people of the territory be consulted to ascertain whether this is what they really want.

Unless, therefore, there is a big change in attitudes toward the remnants of empire on the part of the anticolonial majority, we must expect that proposals by administering powers for retention of a constitutional link between themselves and their dependencies will be viewed with extreme suspicion, and a degree of hostility, at the

United Nations. Particularly among African members, there is a very real difficulty in accepting the proposition that the people of a given dependent territory may simply not want sovereign independence even if it is offered. To many of these members such an attitude is almost incredible.

IV

Any estimate of the impact made by the Committee of Twenty-Four on the process of decolonization must be tentative.[37] Its activities have antogonized the governments of nearly all the administering powers and have earned the plaudits of the majority of members of the United Nations. Since the administering powers are all Western, it has tended to create or widen rifts between Western-aligned and nonaligned countries. Its condemnatory resolutions have, as yet, had no appreciable effect on South Africa, Portugal or the Smith regime in Rhodesia. On the other hand, its activities probably persuaded the Government of Spain to grant independence to Equatorial Guinea and Fernando Po (as the Republic of Equatorial Guinea) in 1968; this step spurred the General Assembly, a few weeks later, to demand that Britain hand over Gibraltar to Spain within a period of months. Some of the administering countries have undoubtedly been moved to quicken progress toward decolonization and to increase economic aid and technical assistance to their remaining dependencies. It is quite possible that the Committee's emphasis on independence was a factor influencing the Nauruans' choice of independence rather than association with Australia. It is also possible that the decision on the British associated states in the Caribbean, with the consequence of permitting opponents of the local leaders to denounce them in New York, may make politicians in other dependent territories more reluctant to agree to association arrangements and may induce the governments of some of the associated states to seek separate independence. Such an outcome would tend to aggravate the problems outlined in the first chapter. And it would introduce more elements of volatility and instability among the Caribbean and Pacific Islands. Of course, if one's top priority is to oust the colonial power, then this is at worst an unfortunate by-product of moral justice and at best a consummation devoutly to be wished.

NOTES

1. The two exceptions were Outer Mongolia, and Singapore which merged with Malaya to become part of Malaysia in 1963, but seceded under duress, becoming a separate independent state in 1965.

2. Resolution 1467(XIV)(1959).

3. Resolution 1542(XV).

4. See generally, *Yearbook of the United Nations for 1960,* 504–513.

5. Cf. Resolution 2353(XXII) (1967), 2.

6. If Britain had been prepared to use force against the Smith regime in Southern Rhodesia, as the General Assembly had insistently demanded, a short period of British colonial rule prior to handing over the reins of government to the African nationalist leaders would probably have been acceptable to the General Assembly. A white minority regime, of course, has no right, inalienable or otherwise, to a grant of independence.

7. See Resolution 2066(XX) (1965). See also Resolution 2105 (XX), §12, on the need to dismantle military bases in colonial territories.

8. See generally Evan Luard (ed.), *The International Protection of Human Rights* (New York: Praeger, 1967). Cf. *Book Review, New York University Journal of International Law & Politics* (1968), 1,131, referring to the "impotent futility" of the Commission.

9. E.g., Resolution 2131(XX) (1965).

10. E.g., Resolution 1803(XVII) (1962).

11. For the Goa incident, see T. B. Millar, *The Commonwealth and the United Nations* (Sydney: Sydney University Press, 1967), 82–90; Quincy Wright, 56, *American Journal of International Law* (1962), 617–632.

12. E.g., Resolution 2326(XXII), §6.

13. Resolution 2353(XXII).

14. It is interesting that only three Commonwealth countries, Pakistan, Zambia, and Tanzania, voted for the resolution, seven, including India, abstained and no fewer than fifteen, including a number of nonwhite members, voted against it. This was the closest approach to Commonwealth "solidarity" with Britain on a colonial problem in recent years.

15. The United States abstained. The Communist countries, with some reluctance, voted in favor of the resolution.

16. If one discounts the Communist, Arab and Latin American votes, the voting figures on the 1968 resolution become twenty-three to eighteen, with thirty-three abstentions.

17. See Resolution 1956(XVIII).

18. Australia decided to withdraw from the Committee in February 1969.

19. See, e.g., Resolution 2326 (XXII) (1967), §17. No general study of small territories has yet been undertaken by the Committee, though a preliminary and inconclusive discussion was undertaken early in 1969.

20. Vividly portrayed in retrospect in James Morris's *Pax Brittanica* (London: Faber, 1968), and echoed by the support given white Rhodesians to Ian Smith and, on an equally disagreeable and widely publicized scale, by some white Americans to George Wallace and some white Britons to Enoch Powell.

21. See J. W. Davidson, *Samoa mo Samoa* (London: Oxford University Press, 1967).

22. The Act was amended in certain respects early in 1965, in response to local pressure. For the consolidated text of the Constitution, see the Cook Islands Constitution Amendment Act (New Zealand, 1965, C.2), Schedule 2. For a synopsis and comment, see de Smith in *Annual Survey of Commonwealth Law, 1965,* ed. H. W. R. Wade (London: Butterworth's Ltd. (1966), 30–35.

23. Document A/5962 (General Assembly, Official Records, 20th session, Annexes, Vol. 1, Item 24).

24. Document A.6000/Rev. 1, VIII, 395.

25. See G.A.O.R., 20th Sess. 4th Cttee., 253-270, 395–409.

26. Resolution 2064(XX)(1965).

27. See further, pp. 77–79, *Post.*

28. For details of the scheme and an analysis of its implications, see Margaret Broderick, 17, *International and Comparative Law Quarterly* (1968), 368–403 (though St. Vincent is there incorrectly listed as being already an associated state).

29. West Indies Act 1967, c. 4 (U.K.), Sched. 2.

30. The discussions are summarized in 4, *United Nations Monthly Chronicle* (March 1967), 25–30 (April 1967), 25–36.

31. In *Status and Problems of Very Small States and Territories* (Unitar Series No. 3), the procedural objection is apparently accepted at its face value (97–100).

32. Chapter and verse are offered in the writer's article, "Mauritius: Constitutionalism in a Plural Society," 31, *Modern L. Rev.,* 601–622 (1968), 612, N.39.

33. See 5, *United Nations Monthly Chronicle* (August–September, 1968), 85–89.

34. See Document A/6868 and Add 1., esp. 35–61 of the Addendum.

35. Resolution 2288(XXII).

36. No effective answer was made to the particularly frank and full statement by the British representative in the Fourth Committee on November 21, 1967 (A/C. 4/SR. 1720, 6–23); see in particular his comment (13–14) that those British colonies in which there had been the most overseas investment had been decolonized first. Cf. the Indian representative's assertion, made shortly afterwards: "The continued dominance of foreign monopolies in collaboration with the colonial power was a universal pattern in colonial territories" (A/C. 4/SR. 1723, 3).

37. For a recent assessment, see Kenneth J. Twitchett, "The Colonial Powers and the United Nations," 4, *Journal of Contemporary History,* (1969), 167–185.

CHAPTER 5

Patternless Islands

Small island, go back where you belong.
You come from Grenada in a fishing-boat,
And now you're wearing a saga-boy coat.
Small island, go back where you belong.
(Trinidadian Calypso)

I

This is best regarded as a politically unscientific essay. Like the Caucus race in *Alice in Wonderland,* it has no determinate beginning or end; and what lies in between is apt to beget confusion. However, as an Irish seafarer might say, "we are entitled to the benefits of serendipity. We may or may not arrive: but the views are splendid and the walk is good exercise." [1]

Authoritative general works on the ecology, sociology and politics of islands are conspicious by their absence. Only the writers of textbooks on geography have the hardihood to offer pronouncements on far-away territories of which they know nothing. In associating myself *ad hoc* with this company I may at least succeed in stimulating thoughts about the political problems posed by the existence of thousands of small islands in the modern world. One of these problems can be stated immediately. Each year the General Assembly of the United Nations passes a number of resolutions calling upon administering countries to implement without delay the provisions of Resolution 1514(XV) in relation to named dependent territories. One of these resolutions lists all those dependent territories not singled out in special individual resolutions. The general resolution for 1967 named twenty-six territories, of which twenty-five were islands or island groups. Of the twenty-six, the one mainland territory (Swaziland) and one insular colony (Mauritius) became independent in 1968. Of the remainder, none had a population of over 150,000, and eight had populations of under 10,000.

II

ISLANDERS AND INSULARITY

In their more romantic moments, the British affect to think of themselves as hardy, seagirt island folk, independent, self-reliant, closely knit, and different from other peoples. And in 1940 this self-image was no chimera. To the lexicographer, islanders are simply insular. The connotations of this adjective tend to be derogatory: narrow-minded, isolated, self-contained, circumscribed, illiberal, prejudiced. Former President de Gaulle, himself in some ways a characteristically insular type, would gladly extend the list.

For anyone wishing to develop this theme at length, there are, of course, powerful disincentives. Australia and Anguilla, Greenland and Guernsey, Iceland and Ireland, the Maldives and Madagascar, Saipan and Sark are islands. What else have they in common with one another? The short answer must be a lemon. Even insularity is a concept of uncertain meaning. In what senses could Japan be said to be insular in 1853, 1945 and 1969, respectively? Is Japan, or Jamaica, or Jersey, more "insular" today than Albania, Bhutan, Sikkim, South Africa, Tibet, or indeed China itself? Is not Poland a striking example of continental "insularity"?

One must concede that islands can be classified in various ways —islands large and small, rich and poor, tropical and temperate, remote and less remote, independent and dependent in status; individual islands and island groups; reasonably homogeneous islands or island groups, and those which are riven by communal strife or threatened by separatist tendencies, or under more than one wholly distinct political regime. Perhaps the most useful classification is one based on regional location. In the Caribbean and the Pacific the similarities, real or apparent, between the island territories in each area are, on the whole, close enough for comparative study to be meaningful, though the dearth of up-to-date and adequate information is a handicap. Later in this chapter we shall touch upon some of the political problems in these two regions. We shall also have something to say about insular separatism and the influence of external factors on the problems of smaller islands. But first the theme of insularity can be pursued farther.

(1) Islands have clearly defined boundaries. Save where an island is divided into alien political units or is psychologically dominated by communal affiliations, its inhabitants tend to have a strong sense of "belonging" to a distinct geographical entity. This does not exclude loyalty to a larger entity (including a mainland territory, or to a group of islands—e.g., the Philippines), but it is apt to generate feelings ranging from local pride to xenophobia. These feelings are not necessarily different in kind or degree from the in-group loyalties of tribal, religious, linguistic or other communal groups in mainland political societies; but by virtue of being expressed within the confines of a visibly separate geographical area they may appear a "legitimate" and even, to the spectator, an attractive manifestation of particularism. Hence, the widespread sympathy with the Anguillans in their revolt against the authority of St. Kitts.

(2) The barrier interposed by a stretch of salt water tends to accentuate and even create cultural or political differences between neighboring territories. This proposition must be stated cautiously. For the relations between some peoples with common land frontiers are excruciatingly bad, and the sea can at least diminish the frequency of abrasive contacts. But it is not difficult to illustrate the general principle. Probably the English differ at least as much in temperament from the Welsh as they do from the French, and Welsh nationalism is now a force to be reckoned with in British politics. Yet the common frontier led to political union, freedom of movement, large-scale intermarriage, a partial Anglicization of Wales and Welsh culture, and the reign of Lloyd George in Downing Street. The English Channel, on the other hand, is wider than the Atlantic Ocean, wider even than the Irish Sea. Again, Madagascar prefers not to think of itself as an authentically African country. Japan, though indubitably Asian, remains unique.

Countries similar in culture may drift apart in the oceans. Both Australia and New Zealand stand in high regard among Western peoples, and they have much in common. But in order to hear either country thoroughly denigrated, one must visit the other. Perhaps one can find a still better example in the Channel Islands. These islands, situated off the northern coast of France, are part of the dominions of the British Crown, dating back to the time when the King of England was Duke of Normandy. They are neither colonies nor integrated with the United Kingdom. They are internally self-governing, and by custom the United Kingdom abstains from interference in their internal affairs except with their concurrence,[2] even though it is responsible for their defense and external relations. Jersey (65,000) and Guernsey (45,000), by far the most populous of the islands, have similar (and very unusual) political institutions, an identical and anomalous constitutional status, broadly common traditions, and geographical proximity to one another. Both enjoy advantageous tax systems; [3] both attract the British tourist; [4] both are English-speaking but with a dwindling background of ancient French *patois*.[5] Relations between them, though, are not wholly harmonious. The islands are "divided by centuries of traditional rivalry, half a joke and half serious. . . ." [6] One reads in a report recently published in Guernsey, that the island

> does not make any pretence of presenting the superficial resort that is so typical in the U.K. So many of the resorts are overcommercialised to the extent that the tourist visiting them must be exploited to a high degree. The present policy behind tourism in Guernsey would not welcome a move towards such a situation even if it were felt that Guernsey was in a position to compete with places such as Blackpool or even Jersey.[7]

The two islands assumed divergent tactical positions at the prospect of Britain's entry into the EEC.[8] While Jersey has sought a redefinition of its constitutional status *vis-à-vis* the United Kingdom, Guernsey showed no interest in such matters till the United Kingdom Government announced its intention, late in 1968, of appointing a commission to consider relationships not only with the regions of the United Kingdom but also with the Channel Islands and the Isle of Man.[9]

Guernsey enjoys the dubious advantage of having the two next largest of the Channel Islands, Alderney and Sark, within its bailiwick. Alderney (population c.1600) is partly self-governing but is substantially a dependency of Guernsey.[10] When things go wrong, it is said that Alderney always blames Guernsey for everything.[11] On Sark (population c.550) the hand of Guernsey has rested lightly; and as long as the octogenarian Dame Sibyl Hathaway, the feudal proprietress of Sark, was with us, Sark, "where time stands still," was certain to remain a picturesque anachronism. Sark still has no income tax, no mechanically propelled vehicles except tractors, invalid carriages and an ambulance (though its inhabitants are understood to muster five privately owned aircraft among them), no divorce laws, no police, sixteen hotels, and a prison to accommodate two. Local attitudes toward Guernsey tend to be less than charitable. When the island was occupied by the Nazis in 1940, many of the natives found the invaders no more foreign than tourists or Guernseymen.[12] Great was the consternation in Sark when, in mid-1969, the Dame of Sark announced her intention of retiring and handing over the administration of the island to Guernsey. They were able to obtain a temporary respite from this disaster when it was pointed out that perhaps the Dame did not, after all, have this ultimate power. No one, not excluding the Dame, was quite sure of the extent of her constitutional authority.

Attitudes such as these are, in one aspect, healthy assertions of individuality. But political chaos is not far away when they are transposed into a Caribbean or Pacific environment.

(3) Special problems tend to cluster about very small and remote island territories. For this purpose a territory is understood to be remote if it does not enjoy adequate and regular communications with a major population center. In Europe there are small continental territories (Luxemburg, Monaco, Liechtenstein, San Marino, the Vatican City and Andorra) and a number of islands small in size or population or both (e.g., Iceland, Cyprus, Malta, the Faroes, the Balearic Isles, Corsica, the Aaland Islands, the Aegean Islands, the Channel Islands and the Isle of Man), but only the Faroes (under Danish sovereignty), some of the Aegean islands and possibly Corsica are remote in this sense. The smaller Himalayan territories can perhaps be regarded as honorary islands, isolated by vast mountain ranges; so, indeed, can the many inaccessible pockets in the interior of New Guinea. The great majority of islands in the Pacific, the South Atlantic and the Indian Ocean are both small and remote. Nearly

all the Caribbean and North Atlantic islands are small; the remoteness of many of them has been diminished by the expansion of air services and tourism during the last decade.

The inhabitants of inaccessible islands usually have a parochial outlook, and they are seldom influenced by the prevailing currents of world opinion. This may be attributed partly to preoccupation with the means of subsistence, partly to lack of incentives to diversify their interests or develop their talents, partly to social and religious pressures toward conformity, partly to the irrelevance of ideologies and the importance of dominant individuals, and partly to the poverty of informative media. To take an extreme example, in 1965 the only newspaper circulating in the Cook Islands, the official Government newssheet, took up to six months to reach some of the outlying islands.[13] These isolated peoples will be ill-informed about world affairs, not necessarily a disaster for them, and the outside world will be ill-informed about them. (Who knew anything worth knowing about Anguilla before 1967? Where is Rodrigues, and why should anybody care?)

This is not to say that they will lack a shrewd appreciation of their own unimportance on the international scene, or of the opportunities that may arise when they are discovered by tourists or strategic planners or the Committee of Twenty-Four. Nor is this to say that they will not heartily detest their nearest neighbors. But to view them through spectacles made on the mainland is to distort reality.

Here we can glance at two small and remote islands, about which a fair amount of information has recently become available. They have been brought into the news by the force of external factors, and ostensibly they have chosen opposite directions; but the inner forces by which their peoples were moved appear to have been basically similar.

Tristan da Cunha lies nearly 2,000 miles offshore in the South Atlantic. It is a dependency of the British colony St. Helena, though government is minimal. In 1961 it had a population of about 300, eking out a bare living in the fishing industry and by subsistence farming and potato growing. The community was closely knit, and neighbors freely offered assistance in building and repairing dwellings and carrying out tasks necessary for survival. But that year disaster struck; a volcano erupted, causing serious damage to land and livestock. After several months the islanders were evacuated en masse to England. They were accommodated in a disused Royal Air Force camp. They were exposed to the English climate, journalists, television cameras and influenza. They found jobs as unskilled laborers. A year later they conducted a secret ballot on the question whether they should return home. All but 5% of them decided to go back to poverty, isolation and good fellowship. The only world these Tristan islanders wished to know was their own.

In many ways this story speaks for itself. Three points ought to be made though. First, the case of Tristan brings out the difficulty of implementing one rational solution to the problems posed by remote and impoverished islands—evacuation and resettlement elsewhere. Second, it illustrates how vulnerable minute islands may be to natural catastrophes—hurricanes, floods, droughts and epidemics are the most typical hazards—that geographically larger territories could withstand. Third, life on Tristan has not been quite the same since the evacuation. Although a new fish-freezing plant has been built and a local broadcasting service started, a number of the younger people, faced with a return to domesticity, yearn for the allurements of urban life, and some have already emigrated.

As Tristan moved back into obscurity, Nauru, a speck in the western Pacific, thrust itself into prominence. It lies just beyond the boundaries of Micronesia, the United States trust territory, to the north, and the Gilbert and Ellice Islands, a British colony, to the east. A former German colony, it was exploited for its rich phosphate deposits. It became a separate mandated territory under Australian administration [14] after the First World War. The German phosphate company was expropriated and a new monopoly, the British Phosphate Commission, owned by the British, Australian and New Zealand Governments, was exchanged for the old. Nauru duly became a trust territory. A Local Government Council with narrow powers was established, but not until 1966 was there a full-fledged Legislative Council. In January 1968, Nauru, an island of eight square miles and 6,000 inhabitants, achieved independence with the highest per capita income of any sovereign state in the world.

This remarkable transition can be attributed above all to the tenacity of a single-minded indigenous leader. Head Chief (now President) Hammer De Roburt was moved not so much by a single-minded devotion to the concept of independence—only a few years ago he had to make inquiries to ascertain the distinction between "self-government" and independence—but by a determination to maintain the identity and integrity of the tiny Nauruan nation. He arrived at the conclusion, in the 1960s, that independence was the best means of achieving that end, and also the most dignified and potentially lucrative of the available options. Nauru's biggest problem was that of being a "self-liquidating island." [15] Before the end of the century the phosphate deposits, on which everything depended, would be exhausted unless the rate of extraction was cut down. United Nations Visiting Missions encouraged the idea of evacuation and resettlement. The Australian Government offered Curtis Island, off the coast of Queensland, as a new home for the Nauruans. In 1964 the offer was rejected, mainly, it seems, because De Roburt felt that his people would be unable to preserve their autonomy and would be absorbed into the Australian community. There followed a period of dexterous arm-twisting. The Nauruans sought a big increase in the royalties paid by the Commissioners, and got it; [16] at the same time they applied pressure for separate independence. During negotiations with the partner governments in 1967, Australia offered an association arrangement along the lines of the Cook Islands scheme but without the option of a unilateral move to independence. This proposal was rejected by the Nauruans, fortified by their status as a trust territory and the atmosphere generated by the Committee of Twenty-Four, which was now calling for Nauruan independence. Australia then offered independence subject to the conclusion of a treaty under which it would conduct Nauru's external relations, or alternatively act as Nauru's agent in external affairs, as New Zealand had acted for Samoa. De Roburt, however, insisted on an unconditional grant of independence.[17] No local referendum was conducted on the issue of independence. The assets of the British Phosphate Commissioners were to be transferred to Nauru upon payment of compensation.

Independence was celebrated, amid general felicitations, on January 30, 1968. Nauru, a true microstate, is to be for the Nauruans, who constitute only half the population.[18] Still basically inward-looking and home-loving, the Nauruans, now wealthy—wealthy enough to acquire a new home when the deposits are exhausted—and comparatively leisured, have preserved themselves and their pride by hacking out a road along which many other small Pacific island peoples would be delighted to follow—if only they could.

III

INSULAR SEPARATISM

Since the Second World War there have been a few instances of island territories voluntarily surrendering or diminishing their separate identity by union with a mainland state. Newfoundland became the tenth province of Canada in 1949; Sarawak and Zanzibar entered into somewhat uneasy federal unions with Malaya and Tanganyika, respectively, in 1963 and 1964. These cases are exceptional. It is interesting that in Cyprus, where the bulk of the population would undoubtedly have preferred union with Greece to independence in 1960, enthusiam for *enosis* has perceptibly cooled.

The general rule is that separate island entities will wish to remain at arm's length from their insular and mainland neighbors. The point has already been sufficiently illustrated by the references to Jersey and Guernsey. And they will normally be resistant to attempts to create new political entities curbing their individual autonomy. Britain's efforts to evoke connubial ardor in the West Indies met with only a half-hearted and transient response.

More serious is the marked tendency toward fragmentation within existing island groups. In the Commonwealth alone during 1968 there were at least five vocal and active insular separatist movements—in Anguilla (St. Kitts-Nevis-Anguilla), Barbuda (Antigua), Rodrigues (Mauritius) and New Britain [19] (Papua–New Guinea), and among the Banabans, formerly of Ocean Island in the Gilbert and Ellice group but now resettled on Rabi Island in the Fiji group.

No one can assess with confidence the dimensions of this problem, but three preliminary points can be made. First, among small territories, several existing island groups (the Bahamas, the Maldives, Fiji, French Polynesia, the Gilbert and Ellice Islands, the New Hebrides, the Ryuku and Bonin Islands, the British Solomon Islands, Tonga, and Micronesia) are known to include thirty or more inhabited islands. It is interesting that most of these groups are in the Pacific. Second, even though the number of islands in a group may be small and the islands substantially homogeneous in culture and language, insularity tends to keep breaking in at the expense of cooperation. This point can be illustrated only too readily in the Caribbean. Third, when a unit in an island group insists on secession (e.g., Jamaica from the West Indies Federation) or purports to secede (e.g., Anguilla), the central government may well find it more difficult, for political reasons or for lack of coercive power, to restrain or reduce the secessionists than if the territory were part of a mainland entity.

Anguilla is the best-known example of insular secession in recent years. The hyphen linking Anguilla, the eel-like island, with St. Kitts and Nevis, looks more than ever like a printer's error. And its rebellion against the authority of St. Kitts, a rebellion preposterous and pathetic, comical and courageous, has dramatized for Americans most of the problems covered in this book.

Anguilla lies some seventy miles to the north of St. Kitts in the Leeward Islands, separated from it by French and Dutch islands. It has about 6,000 inhabitants, women preponderant at any given time because the men are working elsewhere. The soil is poor, and salt is the main product. Lobster fishing, boat building, house construction and subsistence agriculture provide other means of employment. There are as yet undeveloped opportunities for attracting tourists, but basic facilities have been lacking. In 1968 there was one road, no general system of water or electricity, and no telephone system. The sugar and sea-island cotton plantations had gone. But the poverty of the island was relieved by remittances from its emigrant sons, most of whom will return one fine day.

The people of Anguilla tend to be egalitarian but individualistic, politically naive but independent-minded, insular but not altogether inward-looking. Anguilla, though not a homogeneous island—its people are differentiated by color, religion, residential location, personal faction and wealth—is ostensibly united by local pride, and by antipathy toward St. Kittitians in general and Mr. Robert Bradshaw, the Premier of the associated state, in particular.

Anguilla came to be administered under St. Kitts during the nineteenth century, mainly because nobody else wanted it. The island was neglected economically, socially and educationally by Britain and St. Kitts. St. Kitts rather than Britain received the blame. The authority of St. Kitts in Anguilla was represented by a warden who combined administrative with judicial powers, despite Montesquieu. At the St. Kitts-Nevis-Anguilla Constitutional Conference, held in London in May 1966, the principles for the implementation of the associated statehood scheme [20] were agreed unanimously with a delegation including the elected member for Anguilla; [21] and a constitution for a new associated state was brought into effect on February 27, 1967.[22]

However, trouble had already begun. The Anguillans had not been fully alive to the implications of statehood. They had not minded being a British colony; they did mind being governed by Mr. Bradshaw without the interposition of the imperial paternalist as safeguard. When they awoke to the reality of the situation, they were not enthusiastic. At a Miss Associated Statehood beauty contest held on the island, shots were fired (harmlessly); contestants, judges and spectators dispersed precipitately. It was found prudent to raise the new flag of the associated state under cover of darkness. Soon afterward the Warden's house was mysteriously burned. In May the contingent of the state's police force on the island was peacefully rounded up by rebels and summarily deported by aircraft to St. Kitts. In July a referendum was organized on Anguilla and a large majority of the electorate voted for secession. But what the Anguillans wanted at that time was not sovereign independence, but separate colonial status or association, preferably with Britain.

Here, then, was a peculiarly intractable problem.[23] It was embarrassing for the United Kingdom Government, which, having refused to use force against rebellious white Rhodesians, was unwilling to coerce colored Anguillans. The Government first took the view that the matter lay outside the scope of its responsibilities for the defense and external affairs of the associated state because it was essentially an internal security question. This was particularly exasperating for Robert Bradshaw, who had the will but not the means to impose his authority once again upon Anguilla. Mr. Bradshaw, a former trade union leader, energetic, efficient,[24] impatient, imperious, a connoisseur of Georgian antiques, driver of a vintage Rolls Royce and expert in court etiquette and heraldry, held sway in St. Kitts, but his hold over neighboring Nevis, traditional rival of St. Kitts, was tenuous. To allow Anguilla to secede by introducing a constitutional amendment would have had serious repercussions in Nevis.[25] Moreover, he had been affronted, personally insulted and made to look ridiculous, by the Anguillans and their sympathizers. He had aspired to be the Abraham Lincoln of the Caribbean. Instead, he was caricatured and reviled as a Hitler. The Opposition party had espoused the Anguillan cause. His own party was essentially a proletarian party of the "have-nots"; the Anguillans, sturdy individualists, had aligned themselves with the "haves." Immediately after the eviction of the police from Anguilla, a state of emergency was declared. Economic sanctions were directed against Anguilla. Some twenty of Bradshaw's most active opponents, including the opposition leader, were placed in preventive detention, and several others were deported, after shooting incidents (without loss of life) had occurred. Legal flaws were detected, and the emergency regulations were held to be *ultra vires.*[26] New legislation was passed to regularize the emergency. Opposition leaders were put on trial for conspiracy. Attempts were made to intimidate the trial judge and counsel for the defendants; nevertheless the prosecutions failed.[27] The state of emergency was not terminated till well into 1968.[28]

Meanwhile the governments of the four independent Commonwealth countries in the Caribbean—Barbados, Guyana, Jamaica, and Trinidad and Tobago—had moved into action. Political instability, perhaps accompanied by further insular fragmentation, in the Caribbean could have disagreeable consequences for them. Representatives of their governments met with a United Kingdom delegation, a St. Kitts-Nevis delegation and a large group of representatives from Anguilla in Barbados at the end of July 1967. They reached an agreement, under which Anguilla would return to the fold with more local autonomy and economic aid; a small peace-keeping police force would be provided by the Commonwealth governments, to be stationed in Anguilla during the early stages of the reestablishment of constitutional government.[29] But when the Anguillan representatives returned home, those who had signed the agreement were repudiated by their fellow islanders; Jamaica opted out of the peacekeeping force and was followed by the others. The rebellion continued and its opponents were intimidated. Life in Anguilla abounded in anomalies: a case of homicide could not be dealt with because there was no qualified judge or magistrate; the island had a part-time Council of Government, professing a novel form of autonomy, loyal to the Crown, issuing its own postage stamps and running its own airline; money to maintain a rudimentary administration and public services was provided by wealthy mainland sympathizers.[30] A kaleidoscopic group of advisers, expert and amateur, was convened. The Committee of Twenty-Four listened to petitioners from the island. Jeremiah Gumbs, an Anguillan by birth but now an American millionaire resident of New Jersey, became the unofficial and unrecognized Anguillan representative at the United Nations.

Late in 1967 a two-man parliamentary delegation from the United Kingdom visited Anguilla. The secretary to the delegation was Anthony Lee, a British official with experience in colonial administration. By agreement with the St. Kitts Government, he remained for a year in Anguilla, in the somewhat ambiguous capacity of administrative adviser. Phlegmatic, practical, and fair-minded, he established friendly relations with Mr. Ronald Webster, the chairman of the Anguillan Council, during this holding operation. But no one was able to resolve the state of political deadlock. It was so much easier to analyze the problem than to offer solutions, so much easier to offer solutions than to implement them. Opinion in Anguilla hardened in favor of separate independence; but Bradshaw was insistent on restoring the unity of the associated state. In December 1968 Webster announced that Anguilla would become a republic, and called for Lee's withdrawal. The British Government withdrew both Lee and the development aid it was supplying to Anguilla.

In February 1969 the Anguillans purported to adopt, by referendum, a republican constitution, with Ronald Webster as president of the new state. The Commonwealth governments in the Caribbean met, and agreed that the British Government should take such action as was necessary to restore the unity of St. Kitts-Nevis-Anguilla. Mr. William Whitlock, a junior Minister at the Foreign and Commonwealth Office, visited Anguilla early in March. He was greeted with God Save the Queen, Rule Britannia, and a flutter of Union Jacks from the crowd at the airstrip. Soon afterward came shots fired by some of Webster's overzealous supporters. Whitlock made a tactical retreat. A week later, on March 19, three hundred British paratroops were flown into Anguilla to restore law and order. There was no armed resistance. The paratroops were followed by Tony Lee, now "Her Majesty's Commissioner in Anguilla," armed with far-reaching statutory powers.[31]

The combat troops were soon replaced by men from the Royal Engineers, who began to construct public works, and by unarmed

British police. Not a shot was fired in anger—but the political problems remained. Inevitably, the British Government was now ridiculed at home and abroad. Some of the Commonwealth Caribbean governments hastily dissociated themselves from the measures to which they had already agreed in principle. The caricatures of Robert Bradshaw became still more demoniacal. Ronald Webster and his supporters refused to cooperate with Tony Lee, whose position was almost impossible. The Committee of Twenty-Four expressed its grave concern at the armed intervention and called upon Britain to admit a visiting mission; the British representative walked out. The United States representative refused to join in condemning Britain.

On March 28 Lord Caradon, the British Ambassador to the United Nations, flew to Anguilla and reached a seven point agreement with Ronald Webster, which recognized Lee's status and provided for an advisory council of Anguillans. The agreement referred to the British Foreign and Commonwealth Secretary's public statement that "It is not part of [the British Government's] purpose to put [the Anguillans] under an administration under which they do not want to live." Not surprisingly, Robert Bradshaw refused to recognize the validity of this agreement. And soon afterward the predictably unpredictable Webster repudiated it, claiming unconvincingly that he had been "double-crossed." The impasse seemed complete.

Perhaps the situation was desperate. It was hardly serious. The maligned Lee, whose failure to achieve the impossible had been in no way discreditable, left Anguilla in April and returned to an official post in London. The leading Anguillans, often at odds with one another, contrived to cooperative with his successors. British economic aid and the presence of British police were producing results. Bradshaw came to London, received a sizeable financial handout for St. Kitts and Nevis, and went home with a promise that a Commonwealth commission would be constituted by the British Government and his own before the end of 1969 to examine the Anguillan problem on the understanding that Anguilla was part of a unitary state. But there was no sign that the Anguillans would submit voluntarily or be subjected forcibly to effective reunion with St. Kitts. And Britain had divested itself, in 1967, of legal authority to sever the union without the concurrence of the Government of the associated state. All the dilemmas concealed by the concept of associated statehood lay bare.

The attitude of the United Nations toward this issue has been reasonably consistent. The International Covenants on Civil and Political Rights and Economic and Cultural Rights, adopted by the General Assembly in December 1966, began with the affirmation: "All peoples have the right of self-determination." Paragraph 2 of Resolution 1514(XV) embodies similar language. But these affirmations are not to be taken literally. They do not apply to the Katangese, the Baganda, the Southern Sudanese, the Gibraltarians, the Kurds, the Biafrans [32] or the Czechs. Members of the United Nations are, on the whole, staunch supporters of the status quo, except when it comes to decolonization. Even then, as we have already noted,[33] the entire territory is deemed to house a single "people" entitled to collective self-determination.[34] Legitimacy frowns on fragmentation, and the stirring generalities of international declarations and covenants must be viewed in that context. Hence Anguilla has been accorded sympathy but no recognition. The Committee of Twenty-Four and the Fourth Committee have received petitions and heard petitioners for Anguilla, because they still regard the associated state of St. Kitts-Nevis-Anguilla as a British colony; but the "people" of the state were still one because their territorial integrity had to remain inviolate. International practice is unlikely to change unless members are persuaded that an ingenious new solution for the problems of places such as Anguilla can be reconciled with their own interests in rejecting claims to separate self-determination.

A secessionist movement is active in Barbuda, a long-neglected dependency of Antigua. Barbuda, close to Anguilla but more sparsely populated, has even less hope than Anguilla of maintaining a separate identity. There is separatist sentiment as well in the Lesser Grenadines, scattered and tiny dependencies of St. Vincent, artificially separated from Grenada's less neglected dependency, Carriacou.[35]

Soon after the Anguillan rebellion, a separatist movement, potentially still more intractable, emerged far away in the Indian Ocean. Mauritius, a British island colony nearly five hundred miles to the east of Madagascar, was about to hold a General Election. The issue was whether the island should proceed to independence (as its Government wished) or enter instead into an association arrangement with Britain (as the Opposition party wished).[36] At the elections, held in August 1967, the Independence party won a majority. These were the first elections to have been held in Rodrigues, an island dependency of Mauritius, lying three hundred and sixty miles farther out in the Indian Ocean. Mauritius had some 750,000 inhabitants, Rodrigues some 20,000. In Rodrigues the Opposition party's candidates won 97% of the vote. Representatives of Rodrigues, backed by their party, urged the United Kingdom to allow the island to secede from Mauritius. Their preference appeared to be union with the French overseas department of Reunion, to the west of Mauritius. The U.K. rejected their pleas.[37] On independence day, March 12, 1968, the new Mauritian flag was raised and lowered in Rodrigues discreetly in darkness.

There are obvious similarities between Rodrigues and Anguilla. Moreover, Rodrigues, like Anguilla, is a poor island of small proprietors and fishermen,[38] without reasonable services and amenities.[39] It is more inaccessible, more remote and more vulnerable than Anguilla. Unlike Anguilla it has no influential well-wishers or local-born millionaires; nor are there energetic young Americans on hand for temporary attachment. And Rodrigues is divided from Mauritius by politics, religion and race. Mauritius is a plural society.[40] Two-thirds of its inhabitants trace their origins to the Indian subcontinent, and rather more than a quarter are Roman Catholic Creoles; the bulk of the Indo-Mauritian population supported independence and the bulk of the Creoles opposed it. Rodrigues is overwhelmingly Creole and Roman Catholic. The Indian Ocean threatens to become a strategic no-man's land, though Mauritius itself has a defense treaty with Britain.[41] If Rodrigues were to purport to secede from Mauritius, it would be extremely difficult for Mauritius to apply effective coercion unless outside assistance were forthcoming; and there is no guarantee that such aid would be provided. Perhaps the Rodriguans will reconcile themselves to their lot, if only because no more attractive option is available. But the situation is hardly reassuring.

Our last illustration of active insular separatism comes from the Pacific. At the western limit of the atolls comprising the Gilbert and Ellice Islands, lies Ocean Island (or Banaba), a British colony since 1900. Like Nauru, its near Micronesian neighbor, it is a phosphate mine (albeit a smaller and poorer mine) worked by the British Phosphate Commissioners. And the Banabans, though they are less fortunately placed than the Nauruans, wish also to be independent. In December 1945 the Banabans, then barely a thousand strong, agreed to resettlement on Rabi Island, considerably larger than Ocean Island, in the Fiji group.[42] In 1947 they conducted a secret ballot and voted in favor of remaining. They were still the main landowners in Ocean Island and were not prevented from returning there, but they had leased their mineral rights in return for royalties. Payments to the Banabans were subject to taxation by the Gilbert and Ellice Islands Government. And for the other islands in the Gilbert and Ellice group—the least viable of all Britain's colonies, with a bare subsistence economy based on copra and fishing [43]—these sums represented a primary source of revenue. The royalties, geared to those paid to Nauru, rose in the 1960's, and the Banabans, resentful that their distant homeland was the source of support for so many other islands, sought a redistribution of the proceeds. The easiest way of achieving this end was by returning to an independent Ocean Island. Their overtures to the United Kingdom were rejected in 1967 and again in 1968 (though Britain offered £80,000 in development aid for Rabi).[44] They petitioned the Committee of Twenty-Four in 1968, and were given a full hearing. Political activity was at last stimulated within the Gilbert and Ellice Islands.

Local leaders proclaimed their own goal to be independence—but independence as an undivided territory. The Committee of Twenty-Four rebuked the administering authority for doing too little for the Banabans in particular and the Gilbert and Ellice Islanders in general,[45] but gave no support to the separatist ambitions of the two thousand Banabans. At the present rate of extraction, the phosphate deposits may be exhausted by 1980. This will be a sad day for the Banabans, and perhaps a sadder day for the Gilbert and Ellice Islands as a whole, if indeed they remain an undivided island group.[46]

This rather pathetic review of contemporary insular separatism speaks for itself. The desire to secede may be prompted by economic, political or communal grievances, hopes or fears. Political change within the island group or among its neighbors often stimulates latent separatist sentiment. An island's desire to deliver itself from the threat of total domination by forces within the group upon the withdrawal of the imperial power [47] or to emulate its more fortunate neighbors may be a potent divisive factor. And those divisive psychological factors aggravate situations where there seem to be good reasons for separation or divorce.

IV

SOME EXTERNAL FACTORS

As we have noted, the United Nations does not encourage insular separatism. However, its reiteration that sovereign independence is the proper goal for very small dependent territories which, as islands or island groups, already happen to be political entities, is indirectly affecting political thinking on islands now part of existing entities. On what moral grounds can their right to self-determination and independence be denied?

The intrusion of colonial powers into an oceanic area tended to harden divisions among the islands by inhibiting freedom of movement and informal cooperation, and by introducing religious sectarianism and promoting uneven levels of economic development. At the same time, those powers imposed an often artificial cohesion on island groups under their own administration. In retrospect this may appear to have been the least of evils, but the political map of the oceans bears many arbitrary features. As self-government has advanced, the administering powers have left the imprint of their own distinctive constitutional, legal and administrative systems. New local leaders have arisen, often dedicated to the preservation of their personal standing and blinkered by the now familiar imported system.[48] Difficult though it may be to stimulate desire for union among islands exposed to similar patterns of government, it is likely to prove far more difficult where islands have been swept into the modern age along fundamentally divergent routes.

External strategic factors may impede decolonization. Island territories are attractive as bases, staging posts, testing grounds, tracking stations and communication centers. Particularly if an island is small or remote, local resentment of an extraneous military presence may be outweighed by an appreciation of its economic benefit.[49] The United Kingdom still has defense facilities in Cyprus, Malta, Singapore, Mauritius and the Maldives (which are independent), and Bahrain, Ascension and the British Indian Ocean Territory (which are not). Some are already run down and others will be vacated before 1972. Plans to construct an airfield on Aldabra in the British Indian Ocean Territory have been abandoned. And whether Diego Garcia will now be developed as a staging post is doubtful.

The United States, the United Kingdom and France found it convenient to conduct nuclear bomb tests in their remote island dependencies. It is of interest that the French tests in 1968 were carried out in French Polynesia, an overseas territory which does not appear in the United Nations list of non-self-governing territories.

America has major bases in Greenland, Iceland, Bermuda, the Bahamas, the Caribbean Islands and the Pacific. It still occupies the Japanese Ryuku islands, including Okinawa. It retains several bases in the Philippines and is installed in Taiwan. The economy of Guam is heavily dependent on military expenditure. Eniwetok and Kwajalein, among the Marshall Islands in Micronesia, are still used for strategic purposes. And a number of very small islands with no permanent inhabitants (e.g., Midway, Wake) also serve America's military needs.[50] Technological developments, economic crises and political reappraisals lead to frequent changes in appreciations of strategic requirements, but it can be assumed that the United States will at least continue to attach importance to denying potentially hostile foreign powers access to such facilities. The significance of this factor is clear when one considers the future of America's Pacific dependencies.

The use of tiny islands as the objects of nuclear tests conducted by western powers (accompanied, if necessary, by the evacuation of the local population) dramatically emphasizes their subordination and dependence. But small islands and island groups are nearly always dependent on external factors over which they have no effective control: they are often exposed to the force of the elements; their economies, save in very exceptional cases (e.g., Trinidad), are narrowly based, and subject to fluctuations in world demand for primary produce over which they have little or no influence. For each Nauru, Sark or St. Thomas there are a hundred poverty-stricken islands. For some, tourism may be an economic (though seldom a moral) panacea; for others it may be a palliative. It cannot be a cure-all, and in too many cases economic diversification presents insuperable difficulties. In a better world, freedom of migration would answer many of these problems; unfortunately this freedom presupposes a willingness on the part of others to receive migrants. The ill-will shown by a substantial section of British public opinion toward Commonwealth immigrants is a typical rather than an abnormal attitude.

V

THE CARIBBEAN: A SKETCH

In the Caribbean one can find the several characteristics of insularity intermingled with anticolonial influences, the wider concept of self-determination, and other external factors.

The record of colonial powers in this area is discreditable. Most of them came to the Spanish Main in search of plunder or to exclude other powers. The natives were slain or scattered. Negro slavery became pervasive. Natural resources were exploited mainly for the benefit of European settlers and the metropolitan peoples. Scant regard was paid to the social welfare or human dignity of the nonwhite inhabitants till recent years. Yet, despite all the suffering, poverty, rejection and disillusionment, one will find many black Englishmen,[51] black Frenchmen,[52] black Americans, and no doubt black Dutchmen, in the Caribbean. Cultural, educational, political, constitutional and administrative patterns are based on metropolitan models. Some islands have striven to assert a distinct national identity, in itself a new divisive factor.

Among the mainland territories in the region Guatemala, Honduras, Nicaragua, Costa Rica, Panama, Colombia, Venezuela and Guyana are independent states. Surinam (which, like Venezuela, has a boundary dispute with Guyana) remains in an uneasy quasi-federal relationship with the Kingdom of the Netherlands—a relationship shared with the Dutch Antilles (the islands of Aruba, Curaçao, Bonaire, St. Eustatius, Saba, and part of St. Maarten). French Guiana is an overseas department of France. The islands of Martinique and Guadeloupe have the same status. Of the other islands, Cuba and Hispaniola (comprising Haiti and the Dominican Republic) have been independent for many years; few bags could be more mixed. Jamaica and Trinidad became independent in 1962 and Barbados in 1966. Five smaller British island territories having become associated states in 1967, and another in 1969, the only colonies (all British) remaining in the area at the be-

THE EASTERN CARIBBEAN

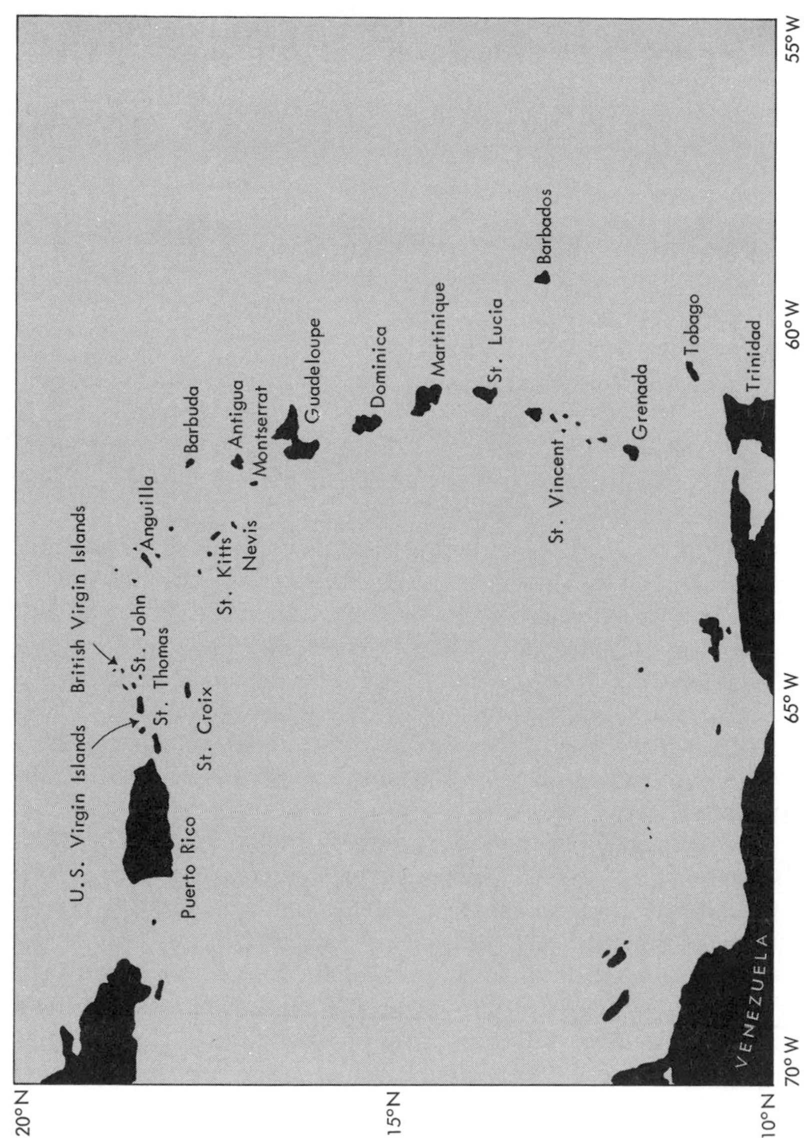

ginning of 1970 were British Honduras, destined for independence, and three very small and poor territories, Montserrat,[53] the British Virgin Islands, and the Cayman Islands, destined for nowhere in particular. Gone are the days when Kipling could write:

> Never was isle so little, never was isle so lone,
> But over the sand and the palm-trees a British flag was flown.

Instead,

> Far-called, our navies melt away;
> On dune and headland sinks the fire.
> Lo, all our pomp of yesterday
> Is one with Nineveh and Tyre!

Of the thirty-one separate political entities in the region, nineteen have populations of under one million; three (all colonies) have fewer than 15,000 inhabitants.[54]

Nobody outside cloud cuckoo land could think of an all-Caribbean federation as a possibility in the near future. The British Honduran politicians' rejection of an American negotiator's proposals for close association between that territory and the contiguous state of Guatemala (to take effect *after* British Honduras had attained independence), shows conclusively that grander designs are pipe dreams. Yet the idea of a federation of Commonwealth islands in the West Indies was not inevitably foredoomed. Why then did it collapse so swiftly?

The answer to this question is fairly complicated.[55] The British Government had initiated proposals for a federal scheme as early as 1945. Procreation took place in 1947, but the period of gestation was preternaturally long, and when the Federation was born, a delicate infant, in 1958, signs of a fatal sickness were already evident. The Federation had no common internal market, no common external tariff and there were restrictions on interisland migration. British Guiana, the British Virgin Islands and British Honduras held themselves aloof from the outset. The Federation was overshadowed by Jamaica and Trinidad, which had a larger measure of self-government than the federation itself, 78% of the population, 84% of the land area and 84% of the revenue. The Federal Government sources of revenue and powers were trivial, and it spent only 3% of the revenues collected in the area.[56] Only in 1960 was internal self-government bestowed on the Federation. The political leaders in Jamaica and Trinidad refused to leave their island power bases in order to take a direct part in federal politics in which only one man could come out on top; they were on bad terms with one another and with the federal leadership. At the first (and only) federal elections the Federal Labour party won a narrow majority, but its candidates in Jamaica and Trinidad fared poorly, which meant that the eight smaller islands had to be given disproportionate representation in the Federal Government. Jamaica felt that its interests were not being adequately safeguarded, particularly as its numerical preponderance was not reflected in the allocation of seats in the Federal Legislature. The other islands resented Jamaica's wish to exercise a dominating influence. In 1961, when the criteria for accession to independence within the Commonwealth had been relaxed (following the admission of Cyprus and Sierra Leone), the Jamaican electorate opted at a local referendum for secession and separate independence. The United Kingdom Government gave way, notwithstanding protests from the other islands. In January 1962 Dr. Eric Williams in Trinidad, declaring that ten minus one equalled zero, announced that his country would follow suit. All that remained for the British Government was to pronounce the obsequies over the amputated patient.

At once a "little eight" began to emerge from the ashes of the dead federation, and a new federal scheme was prepared. The British Government would probably have preferred the remaining islands to enter into a unitary relationship with Trinidad, but it was unwilling to supply the dowry. Wrangles developed among the eight: Grenada, hoping for union with Trinidad, withdrew from the scheme; in 1965 first Antigua, then Montserrat, and finally the largest prospective unit, Barbados, took their leave; and the islands went their separate ways. Only if a very large and continuing financial commitment had been arranged by the British Government at an early stage could the project have gotten off the ground.[57]

Given that the islands had a large measure of linguistic, ethnic and cultural homogeneity, and similar political institutions, these failures are depressing. Anticolonialist sentiment, though patchy, was significant and there was a widespread desire for full autonomy. The British, Federal and island governments devoted an enormous amount of time to devising an acceptable constitutional structure. But enthusiasm for the principle of federal union was apt to cool rapidly when its practical implications were examined. There was too little willingness on the part of the island leaders to accept compromises or jeopardize local economic and political interests for the benefit of a larger entity. Nor was it obvious what positive gains (e.g., obtaining direct economic benefits, or better safeguards against immediate external dangers) would be achieved for the largest islands by a partial submergence of their identity. Indeed, insular particularism was deep-rooted and tenacious. Fellow feeling, a sense of belonging to the British West Indies as a whole, was not strong. West Indians often used to make the sardonic remark that their sole symbol of cultural identity was their cricket team; and this has survived political fragmentation.[58] This dearth of fellow feeling cannot be explained merely by pointing out that West Indian culture is largely derivative; so is Australia's. The salt-water gaps between the West Indian islands, and their long history of separate political development and of dependence on a remote metropolitan power, must be the most likely explanations. Again, till the early 1960s interisland communications were on the whole poor. Trade and travel routes led mostly to the mother country, and the peoples of the islands were not likely to generate active enthusiasm for political union with islands with which they were unacquainted. But the significance of this factor may have been overrated. Political leaders knew one another and were not always favorably impressed. There is often a marked hostility between neighboring islands in the same political grouping (e.g., Nevis and St. Kitts,[59] Barbuda and Antigua, the Grenadines and St. Vincent, St. Thomas and St. Croix).[60] Jamaicans in search of employment on other islands with struggling economies were seldom made to feel welcome. The calypso quoted at the beginning of this chapter bluntly express the prevailing attitude in Trinidad and Tobago toward their closest neighbor.[61] There is little evidence that the increase in movement between the islands during recent years [62] has aroused real interest in political union.[63]

Other factors militated against the creation of a durable union: an uneven distribution of wealth among the islands, conflicts of economic interest and the familiar phenomenon of acrimonious competition for scarce resources. Another important factor, already hinted at, was the style and structure of politics. In substance the federal political parties were no more than loose coalitions of distinct island parties. Many of these parties had charismatic leaders who appealed to the faithful by way of demagogery at mass open-air meetings in a context of purely local issues.[64] This special manifestation of insularity not only impaired personal relationships in federal politics but also helps to explain why the plan for a "little eight" collapsed.

So many schemes for close political integration having gone agley, the immediate outcome was more political separatism—independence for Barbados, associated statehood for others—while the little British Virgin Islands were granted their own ministerial system and, farther to the north, the Bahamas and Bermuda moved along the road to complete autonomy. But the will to cooperate in matters of common concern was not dead, and dreams of a larger political grouping still lingered. There remain some supranational institutions: the University of the West Indies, common meteorological and shipping services, a common Court of Appeal for the Associated States. Ad hoc arrangements have been made for joint diplomatic representation overseas (e.g., the High Commissioner for Guyana also represents Barbados in London) and for joint representation at international conferences. From time to time meetings of the governments of the independent Commonwealth countries in the area are held, and representatives of the associated states, British Honduras and the Bahamas may be invited. Meetings of the West Indies (Associated States) Council of Ministers take place regularly. Still more interesting, if only as a gesture indicating a desire to develop functional links, has been the creation, in May 1968, of a Free Trade Area (CARIFTA), embracing all the British territories in the region (except the British Virgin Islands) and the Bahamas. But plans for a Regional Development Bank were temporarily thwarted by Jamaican noncooperation. Guyana, on the other hand, formerly the least cooperative, now tends to make the running in matters of functional cooperation.[65]

Elsewhere in the region, cooperation and even formal contact between the British and non-British territories in the region are tenuous. The international Caribbean Commission is defunct. The main direct link appears to lie between Jamaica and America's associated state, the Commonwealth of Puerto Rico. Most of the Central American republics have formed a common market (CENTCOM),[66] though none of the independent Commonwealth countries belongs to it. Nor do they belong to the Latin American Free Trade (LAFTA). They are members of the United Nations Economic Commission for

Latin America (ECLA), and the British associated states were recently admitted to joint membership. But ECLA, though a useful clearing-house and source of information, is Latin oriented and offers British territories few positive advantages. A separate Economic Commission for the Caribbean might bring benefits to some Common wealth countries, but the idea would not be popular in Guyana, which is trying to improve diplomatic relations with its Latin neighbors. Hitherto Guyana, unlike Trinidad and Barbados, has been unable to obtain admission to the OAS.

One or two Commonwealth countries in the region, notably Guyana, have received substantial assistance directly from United Nations agencies on an individual basis. In this context they are competitors rather than collaborators, and most of them have a weak bargaining position. This has perhaps been the saddest effect of the collapse of the West Indies Federation and the failure of the little eight.[67] They also compete with one another for private industrial development and for tourists. Jamaica, Barbados, Antigua and now even St. Kitts have enjoyed some success, while others have languished. But they are not in a strong position to compete with the American Virgin Islands and Puerto Rico, which enjoy highly favorable economic arrangements with the United States and offer great attractions to American tourists. Nor are they as fortunate as the French and Dutch territories. The former are integrated with France, and the living standards in all of them are assisted by association agreements with the EEC. To a large extent the Commonwealth countries in the region remain at the mercy of uncertain external factors: world commodity prices, the future of Commonwealth preference and the Commonwealth sugar agreement, British and American financial and immigration policies, the routes of hurricanes, even in some cases the activities of private gambling syndicates. And the smaller the territory, the greater, in general, is its vulnerability.

VI

THE PACIFIC: A SKETCH

In terms of power factors, the Caribbean is still preeminently an American sea. The influence of the United States may be less overwhelming since the intrusion of Castro, and its tenure of the leased Panama Canal Zone is not wholly secure. But America has recently conducted successful military interventions in the internal affairs of Guatemala and the Dominican Republic and, despite the fiasco of the Bay of Pigs, it still has a base in Cuba. In the Pacific, American dominance is neither comprehensive nor assured. On the western seaboard lie two giants, Russia and Communist China. For much of 1942 the outstanding military and naval power in the Pacific was not America but Japan. Japan, conquered at enormous cost, now lies dormant as a military force, with Okinawa increasingly restive under American occupation, and with former mandated islands under American rule. Neighboring Korea was the scene of a bloody ideological war in the early 1950s; in Indonesia the posturing of Sukarno ended with appalling counterrevolutionary carnage in the mid-1960s; in Vietnam the United States became embroiled in a cruel and profitless civil war. ANZUS, SEATO, and an irregular chain of bases and insular possessions have not been enough to give America a sense of security in the Pacific.[68]

The small islands of the Pacific are, on the whole, smaller, poorer, more remote, dispersed and vulnerable, more inward-looking and politically more divided than the Caribbean islands. There are indeed wealthy islands (Nauru, and Oahu in the Hawaiian islands), and others where poverty is not widespread (e.g., New Caledonia, Guam, Tahiti, American Samoa, Viti Levu in Fiji, Saipan in Micronesia). But poverty in a precarious subsistence economy is the common lot in Oceania, and overpopulation has begun to increase the problem for many isolated communities. On the other hand, tourism offers new hope of economic benefits for some islands. Perhaps none will emulate Hawaii (or suffer the same inundation) but Fiji and French Polynesia have already begun to bolster their economies in this way. Other territories, notably Micronesia, are already in the race. New airfields have been laid down in improbable places (e.g., Niue, Tonga, the Cook Islands, Ponape). And there is a dramatic increase in air travel both among the islands and between some islands and the larger countries in the region. A new factor may have far-reaching effects on the economies of some far-flung island groups—the discovery of rich resources lying beneath the ocean bed. Unless an international regime to control the exploitation of these resources is established (as Malta has recently proposed [69]), this factor may make certain administering authorities more reluctant to relinquish political control over scattered island territories which are now heavy economic liabilities.

Ethnically or culturally the small islands fall into three main groups: [70] Micronesians (e.g., in most of the American Trust Territory and the Gilberts), Polynesians (e.g., in Hawaii, the Ellice Islands and Samoa) and Melanesians (e.g., in Fiji and the Solomons). This is, of course, an oversimplification: in Hawaii the largest single ethnic group is Japanese, and in Fiji it is Indian.

The political map of the Pacific is haphazard, a relic above all of the fatal impact of the West [71]—first as navigators, traders, whalers, blackbirders, carriers of strange diseases, missionaries, colonizers and administrators; then during the Second World War, as warriors. If one disregards the islands under the administration of Latin American countries or almost contiguous mainland countries, the islands fall into the following categories:

The Philippines, Western Samoa, Nauru: independent states.
Cook Islands: state in free association with New Zealand.
French Polynesia, New Caledonia, Wallis and Futuna Islands: French overseas territories.
Tonga: internally self-governing British protected state.
Fiji, Pitcairn, Gilbert and Ellice Islands, British Solomon Islands: British dependencies.
New Hebrides: British-French condominium.
Niue, Tokelau Islands: New Zealand possessions.
Papua–New Guinea: part Australian territory, part Australian trust territory, administered as one.[72]
Hawaii: a state of the Union, an integral part of the United States.
American Samoa, Guam: unincorporated territories of the United States.
Micronesia: United States Trust Territory of the Pacific Islands.

There are also miscellaneous minuscule islands under British or American rule.

Regional cooperation is even less developed in the Pacific than in the Caribbean. The South Pacific Commission, whose reach now extends to Guam and Micronesia north of the Equator, does useful work by promoting social and economic research and development and facilitating occasional contacts at annual conferences between

THE PACIFIC ISLANDS

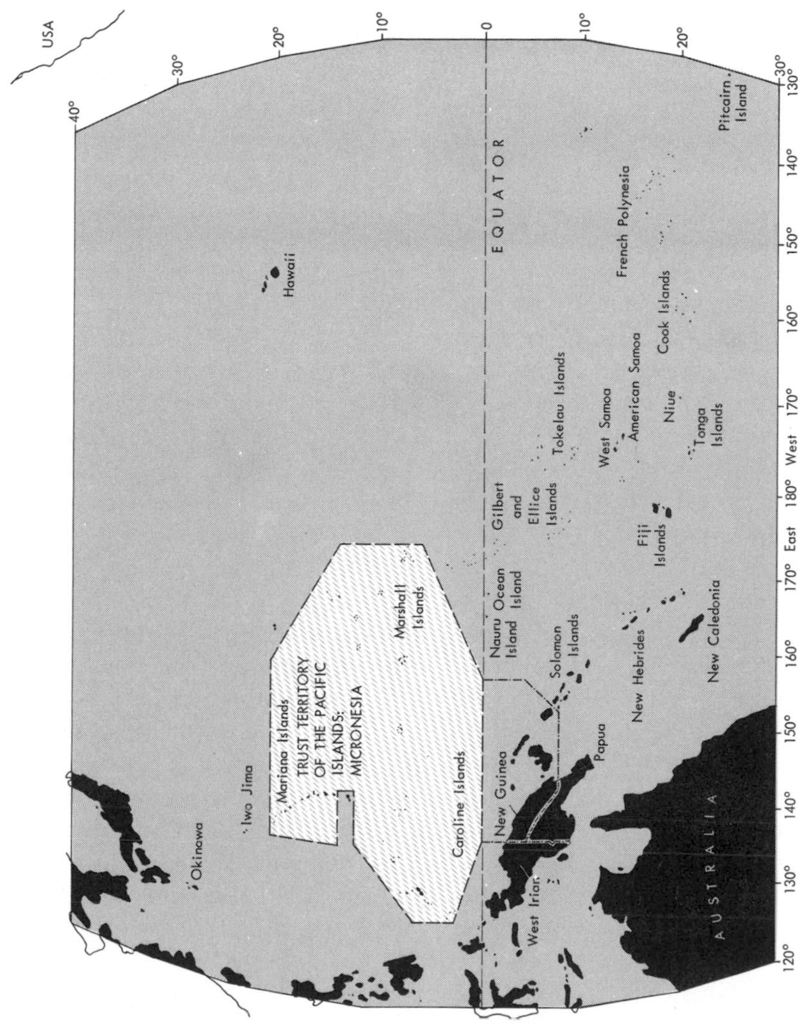

leading politicians and administrators on the various islands. But it is dependent for its funds on the administering authorities, which have been far from lavish.[73] International rivalry in the Pacific now tends to take the form of the cold shoulder. The most absurd illustration of noncooperation is to be found in the New Hebrides, where the co-domini, Britain and France, have implanted their own separate cultures, Resident Commissioners, and legal systems.[74] A more serious anomaly is political apartheid in Samoa. Both Western Samoa and American Samoa agree on the principle of Samoa for the Samoans,[75] an attitude dismally exemplified in 1967 by the Council of Chiefs' advice to the Governor of American Samoa to refuse permission to a Korean fisherman to marry a Samoan woman.[76] But it seems that each Samoa must now be for its own Samoans. Western Samoa would not be anxious to incorporate a small American territory that would become an economic liability if the United States were to withdraw financial support. American Samoa, having comfortably surpassed its neighbor in per capita income in the 1960s, looks to closer links with the United States, the source of largesse and an open door for its surplus population; and the local chiefs shrink from the prospect of a diminution of status upon merger with the higher ranking Western Samoans.[77]

The Pacific islands remain the last of the non-European areas dominated by western administering authorities. They have been insulated and isolated from the main currents of international political opinion. Only in the last decade has there been any significant interest in autonomy. Even today feelings about independence remain ambivalent. Those who seek self-government are often no more radical or outward-looking in their social attitudes than those whose apathy or sense of dependence or fear of the unknown incline them toward acceptance of the status quo or of a slow rate of constitutional development. It is impossible as yet to assess the repercussions of Nauru's accession to independence. It may well encourage Tonga to travel the same road; [78] it has stimulated separatist tendencies among the Banabans of Rabi (and formerly of Ocean Island); [79] it has made an impact on thinking in Micronesia; [80] it may have been partly responsible for the growth of political unrest in French Polynesia.[81] More generally, the anticolonial crusade waged at the United Nations has had some impact on political attitudes in the islands. Resolutions passed in New York demanding independence on the basis of "one man, one vote, one value" have been deeply resented by most of the indigenous Fijians, who are outnumbered by the Indo-Fijian population.[82] It must not be assumed, however, that the effect of these resolutions has been wholly counterproductive. We have noted that the petition of the Banabans to the Committee of Twenty-Four at last bestirred Gilbert and Ellice Islanders to consider their own political future. Even in Australian New Guinea, too fragmented for an effective independence movement, the persistent prodding of the administering authority by the United Nations has indubitably accelerated progress towards internal self-government. But one's tentative prediction must be that demands for self-government and independence will be expressed in the language of insular separatism more frequently than that of territorial integrity.

Because of the dearth of grass roots agitation on the islands, the attitudes of the several administering powers toward the question of independence for their wards have seldom been made explicit, and it would almost certainly be a mistake to imagine that all the metropolitan governments have clearly formulated policies on this matter. That France has no present intention of relinquishing its mission in the Pacific and leaving the ocean to the Anglo-Saxons is clear enough.[83] Manifest destiny has beckoned America to its island paradises,[84] in Hawaii, Guam and Samoa, and there it will stay; but there is no facile solution to the challenge of Micronesia. New Zealand, having shed Western Samoa and accommodated the Cook Islands, remains saddled with Niue and the pathetic Tokelau Islands, trying in vain to convince the United Nations that the people of these tiny territories actually do not want independence. Australia, irked by the United Nations (it has recently withdrawn from the Committee of Twenty-Four), cajoled into granting independence to Nauru, and glancing uneasily at West Irian (which was being incorporated into Indonesia toward the end of 1969, after a formal show of self-determination, with the sanction of the United Nations), is conscious of its own isolated position and need for security.[85] It is unlikely to champion the cause of independence for territories in the Southwest Pacific which might fall under the influence of potentially hostile powers. Britain's general policy is one of decolonization, but this does not yet embrace the concept of independence for Pitcairn. Its attitude toward its Pacific dependencies will doubtless be pragmatic, taking into account first and foremost local opinion, and then such factors as the views of the United States and Australia, the dangers of an outbreak of civil strife in Fiji, and the possible advantages of association rather than independence for its most vulnerable colonies.

NOTES

1. W. J. M. Mackenzie, *Politics and Social Science*. (London: Pelican, 1967), 326. For an able and informative essay, overlapping with the subject matter of this chapter, see D. P. J. Wood, "The Smaller Territories: Some Political Considerations," *Problems of Smaller Territories* (University of London, Athlone Press, 1967), 23–34.

2. To the general rule there are some minor exceptions and one of more consequence: local legislation requires the approval of the Privy Council, an organ of the United Kingdom Government.

3. Income tax is at the rate of 20%; there is no surtax, corporation tax or succession duty.

4. Guernsey had 221,000 visitors staying for three or more days in 1967—a figure comfortably surpassed by Jersey.

5. In Guernsey the visitor will be greeted by the advertisement: *"Guinness est bouanne pour té."* Jersey French is not identical to Guernsey French.

6. Alan Wood and Mary Seaton Wood, *Islands in Danger* (London: New English Library, 1965), 18.

7. *Billet d'Etat,* October 25, 1967, 494–495 (report of the European Free Trade Association and Economic Community Committee, States of Guernsey).

8. Cf. *Jersey and European Economic Community* (States of Jersey, 1967).

9. The Isle of Man's constitutional status is similar to that of the Channel Islands, but it enjoys a somewhat less ample measure of internal autonomy. It has one of the most ancient legislatures in the world. Recently the Manx authorities were engaged in a constitutional and political dispute with the U.K. Government on the question of jurisdiction over pirate radio broadcasting.

10. See generally, *A Short History and Guide to Alderney* (Guernsey Press Co., 1968).

11. Wood and Wood, *op. cit.,* 18, 19, 40, 66.

12. Michael Marshall, *Sark* (Guernsey Press, 1961), 45. See also Wood and Wood, *passim,* for the curious story of Sark in the years of occupation.

13. Report of the United Nations Supervisor of Elections in the Cook Islands (A/5962, §122 [G.A.Off.Rec., 20th Sess., 1965, Annexes, Vol. 1, Item 24]).

14. The British Empire was the Mandatory; the Commonwealth of Australia was entrusted with the administration of the Island. Similar arrangements were continued under the trusteeship system; the United Kingdom, New Zealand and Australia replaced the "British Empire."

15. David W. Wainhouse, *Remnants of Empire* (New York: Harper & Row, 1964), 94. Mr. Wainhouse's monograph, published under the auspices of the Council on Foreign Rela-

tions and subtitled *The United Nations and the End of Colonialism,* is a particularly good survey of the general field.

16. See Nancy Viviani, "Nauru Phosphate Negotiations," 3, *Journal of Pacific History* (1968), 151–153.

17. Why was De Roburt so insistent on unfettered sovereignty, when he had no intention that Nauru should play a full part in international relations and intended that Nauru should retain closer relations with Australia than any other country? His approach was certainly pragmatic; it was not rooted in the usual *a priori* ideological assumptions. After having interviewed De Roburt and others, I am still not clear whether any single factor was decisive, but my impression is that among the most important factors were irritation at the sluggish pace of constitutional advancement and of the negotiations about increasing the phosphate royalties to be paid to the Nauruans; the geographical remoteness of Australia from Nauru and Nauru's economic strength, which made it less dependent on the good will of Australia than were the Cook Islands on New Zealand; and the feeling that unfettered independence would give Nauru greater freedom of maneuver both in dealing with its other Pacific neighbors and in striking a good bargain if and when evacuation of the island became necessary. De Roburt's hand was strengthened by United Nations attitudes, by the rejection of the British scheme for association in the Caribbean as an authentic means of decolonization, and probably by the presence of New Zealand among the partner governments with whom he was negotiating. See further, J. W. Davidson, "The Republic of Nauru," 3, *Journal of Pacific History* (1968), 145–150.

As we have noted (p. 14, *ante*), Nauru became a special member of the (British) Commonwealth in November 1968. This entitles Nauru to play a full part in Commonwealth relations except at meetings of Commonwealth Heads of Government. If De Roburt had been swayed by considerations of prestige and status he would not have agreed to this sensible arrangement, which happens to be much the same as that adopted for the British associated states in the Caribbean.

18. As well as 3,000 Nauruans there were about 1,500 other Pacific islanders (mostly from the Gilbert Islands), 1,100 Chinese (nearly all from Hong Kong) and 400 Europeans in Nauru at the time of independence. The vast majority of employed Nauruans were working in nonmanual jobs; extraction of the phosphates were left to others. Under the Constitution (see Rowena Armstrong, 41, *The Parliamentarian* [1968], 259–261) it is very difficult for persons not belonging to the Nauruan Community to acquire citizenship and qualify for the franchise.

19. See *The Times* (London), October 25, 1968, p. 5, referring to the foundation of the Melanesian Independence Party, which hoped to bring about the secession of the outer islands of the Australian trust territory of New Guinea by 1975. The trust territory itself is multitribal, multilingual (some seven hundred languages have been identified), with poor internal communications and an undeveloped attachment to the ideal of nationhood. The areas designated for "secession" earn over 60% of the export income of Papua and New Guinea. The administering authority will, of course, resist this movement. The case for secession (and union with the British Solomon Islands Protectorate) is put by Leo Hannet in 4, *New Guinea* (June–July 1969), 8–14.

20. U.K. Parliamentary Papers, Cmnd. 2865(1965).

21. *Ibid.,* Cmnd. 3031(1966).

22. U.K. Statutory Instruments 1967, No. 228, made under powers conferred by the West Indies Act 1967.

23. The problem is thoroughly explored in unpublished papers delivered at the Conference on "Anguilla: a Significant Caribbean Revolution" (Puerto Rico: CISCLA, Inter-American University, March 1968). Shorter surveys have appeared in various periodicals: e.g., John Updike, "Letter from Anguilla," *New Yorker* (June 22, 1968), 70.

24. He had been the able Finance Minister in the Government of the defunct West Indies Federation.

25. Both Nevis and Anguilla had indicated a desire to secede in 1958. Mr. Bradshaw's party which carried all seven seats on St. Kitts at the last elections for the Legislative Council (now the House of Assembly) before statehood, put up no candidate for the two seats in Nevis or the seat in Anguilla.

26. *Charles* v. *Phillips & Sealey,* 10 West Indian Reports 423 (1967): *Herbert* v. *Phillips & Sealey, ibid.,* 435.

27. For a critical account of this phase, see *Bulletin of the International Commission of Jurists,* No. 33 (March 1968), 26–30.

28. When I visited St. Kitts in January 1968, all public gatherings other than those for religious purposes and funerals were prohibited under emergency regulations. On the day of my arrival I witnessed a funeral attended by several hundred people.

29. U.K. Parliamentary Papers, Cmnd. 3433(1967).

30. Among Anguilla's active proponents and fund-raisers was Dr. Leopold Kohr, whose amusing work, *The Breakdown of Nations* (London: Routledge & Kegan Paul, 1957), had extolled the virtues of fragmentation.

31. Anguilla (Temporary Provision) Order 1969 (Statutory Instruments 1969, No. 371), made under section 7(2) of the West Indies Act 1967. The Order recited in its preamble that it was made with the concurrence of the Government in St. Kitts, and for the purpose of restoring law and order in Anguilla and preserving the integrity of the associated state so as to ensure that the discharge of the United Kingdom Government's responsibilities for the defense and external affairs of the associated state were not prejudiced. There was a good deal of controversy in Britain over the justification for armed intervention and the scope of the powers asserted.

For a factual synopsis of the events from December 1968, see *Keesing's Contemporary Archives* 23360–23363 (May 17–24, 1969).

32. On the acutely difficult issues involved in applying the concept of self-determination in Nigeria, see K. W. J. Post, 44, *International Affairs* (1968), 26–39, S. K. Panter-Brick, *ibid.,* 254–266.

33. See p. 45, *ante.*

34. For the best discussion of this problem, see Rupert Emerson, *Self-Determination in the Era of Decolonization* (Harvard University Center for International Affairs, 1964). See also Walter Connor, "Self-Determination—the New Phase," 20, *World Politics* (1967), 30; M. A. Shukri, *The Concept of Self-Determination in the United Nations* (Damascus: Al Jadidah Press, 1965), and more generally, Alfred Cobban, *The Nation State and National Self-Determination* (London: Collins, 1969), and Elie Kedourie, *Nationalism* (Praeger, 1961), V–VII.

35. Gordon K. Lewis, *The Growth of the Modern West Indies* (London: MacGibbon & Kee, 1968), 335–337.

36. At a Constitutional Conference held in London in September 1965, the British Secretary of State for the Colonies had expressed his view that it was right that Mauritius should become independent, provided that a newly elected Legislative Assembly so resolved (U.K. Parliamentary Papers, Cmnd. 2797 [1965], 7).

37. See *The Times* (London), January 13, 1968.

38. Mauritius, like St. Kitts, is a sugar island. Rodrigues lives by keeping livestock, growing vegetables and maize, fishing and emigration to Mauritius, and is economically dependent on Mauritius, itself in financial straits.

39. Cf. Quentin Keynes, "Island of the Dodo," 109, *National Geographic Magazine* (1956), 77, 93, 99, 102–104. The picture has not greatly changed since this article was written.

40. See generally Burton Benedict, *Mauritius: Problems of a Plural Society:* (London: Pall Mall Press, 1965); de Smith, 31, *Modern Law Review* (1968), 601–622.

41. U.K. Parliamentary Papers, Cmnd.3629(1968).

42. Ocean Island is a circle, three miles in diameter.

43. The population of the colony (scattered over two million square miles of sea but with a land area of only 370 square miles) in 1968 was about 55,000. Most of the workers in the phosphate operations on Ocean Island and many of those on Nauru are Gilbertese.

44. See 747 U.K. House of Commons Debates, cols. 1247–1258 (June 7, 1967). In 1967 the United Kingdom Government gave the Gilbert and Ellice Islands colony £474,000 (just over $1 million) in aid. The distribution of phosphate revenues between the colony and the Banabans was in the proportion of five to one. The population ratio is some twenty-five to one.

45. See 5, *United Nations Monthly Chronicle* (August–September 1968), 89–93; (November 1968), 24.

46. To some extent they are an artificial entity. The Gilbertese (like the Banabans) are Micronesians; the Ellice Islanders, who constitute about 15% of the population, are Polynesians. Relations between the energetic Ellice Islanders and the more leisurely Gilbertese tend to be strained.

47. The same phenomenon may, of course, occur in a well-defined area in a mainland territory as decolonization reaches its climax (e.g., Ashanti, Buganda, Katanga, Barotseland); or where a territory composed partly of an offshore island and partly of a continental mass proceeds to independence; thus, the new Republic of Equatorial Guinea, consisting of the relatively wealthy island of Fernando Po and an impoverished mainland area, Rio Muni, is already threatened by a secessionist movement in Fernando Po, where in September 1968 a majority had voted against independence: *The Economist,* January 4, 1969, pp. 20–21.

48. Cf., the impracticability of achieving political union between two contiguous states in Africa, Senegal and The Gambia, one francophonic and one anglophonic. It is true that the Southern Cameroons, a trust territory, formerly administered as part of Nigeria, opted for federal union with the French-speaking republic of Cameroon in 1961. This precedent has not been followed anywhere else in Africa. The union between Tanganyika and Zanzibar (Tanzania, 1964) was between English-speaking countries. This too was an exceptional case, comparable with the union of the former British Somaliland Protectorate with Somalia in 1960.

49. Cf. Philip M. Allen, "Self-Determination in the Western Indian Ocean," *International Conciliation* No. 560 (November 1966).

50. See further, Herold J. Wiens, *Pacific Island Bastions of the United States* (New York: Van Nostrand, 1962).

51. In St. Thomas, in the American Virgin Islands, a black Anguillan worker said to me: "You're from England, aren't you? I'm English myself." He had never undergone the sobering experience of a trip to England.

52. Though Frantz Fanon came from Martinique. There is a well-known Martiniquan saying, *peau noir, masque blanc* (black skin, white mask): Fanon adopted it as the title of his first book.

53. For details of the proposals, see K. R. Simmonds, "The Belize Mediation," 17, *International and Comparative Law Quarterly* (1968), 996–1009. The prevailing political and social atmosphere in Guatemala (see Henry Giniger, "Guatemala is a Battleground," *The New York Times Magazine,* June 16, 1968, p. 14), almost comparable with Haiti, did not encourage the British Hondurans to agree to a closer relationship.

54. For general surveys of the area, see Sir Harold Mitchell, *Caribbean Patterns* (Edinburgh: Chambers, 1967), and *Contemporary Politics and Economics in the Caribbean* (Athens: Ohio University Press, 1968).

55. For the fullest account, see Sir John Mordecai, *The West Indies and the Federal Negotiations* (Geo. Allen & Unwin, 1968). See also J. H. Proctor, Jr., "Constitutional Defects and the Collapse of the West Indian Federation" [1964], *Public Law,* 125–151; Gordon K. Lewis, *op. cit.,* note 35, *ante,* XIV, XV.

56. R. D. Watts, *New Federations: Experiments in the Commonwealth* (London: Oxford University Press, 1966), 362, 367.

57. Sir Arthur Lewis, *The Agony of the Eight* (Bridgetown, Barbados, 1966).

58. For this purpose the West Indies include Guyana. They were the unofficial world cricket champions till their surprising defeat by England in the test series in 1968.

59. In the first federal executive body two Ministers were therefore appointed from St. Kitts-Nevis-Anguilla (one from St. Kitts and one from Nevis) despite the smallness of the colony: Watts, *op. cit.,* 276.

60. Cf. Whitney D. Perkins, *Denial of Empire* (Leyden: Sythoff, 1962), 168.

61. Sir Philip Sherlock, *The West Indies* (London: Thames & Hudson, 1966), 97.

62. In St. Kitts-Nevis-Anguilla, a territory of about 58,000 inhabitants, there were over 24,000 arrivals and 25,000 departures (excluding cruising and transit passengers) in 1966; the great majority came from or went to other Caribbean islands. See *Annual Report of the Royal St. Christopher-Nevis-Anguilla Police Force 1966,* Tables 1–6.

63. Although there may be as many Anguillans working in the American Virgin Islands as there are resident in Anguilla itself, no significant body of Anguillan opinion in Anguilla in 1968 seemed to favor union with the American territory. The British Virgin Islands are almost a commuter suburb of their American counterpart, but local sentiment in favor of union has probably weakened of late.

64. See Morley Ayearst, *The British West Indies* (New York: New York University Press, 1960), IX.

65. This is no doubt largely explained by the ethnic composition of the Guyanese population. The largest single element in the community is East Indian, and most of its votes go to the militant People's Progressive party, led by a Marxist, Dr. Cheddi Jagan. The present Government, under Dr. Forbes Burnham, rests predominantly on Negro support.

66. K. R. Simmonds, "The Central American Common Market," 16, *International and Comparative Law Quarterly* (1967), 911–945; Joseph S. Nye, Jr., "Central American Regional Integration" (*International Conciliation,* No. 562, March 1967).

67. Cf. Sir Arthur Lewis, *op. cit.,* 18.

68. Cf. Thomas R. Adam, *Western Interests in the Pacific Realm* (New York: Random House, 1967); Herold J. Wiens, *Pacific Island Bastions of the United States* (New York: Van Nostrand, 1962).

69. Arvid Pardo, "Sovereignty under the Sea: the Threat of National Occupation," *The Round Table* (London), No. 232 (October 1968), 341–355. Dr. Pardo, the Maltese Ambassador to the United Nations, has made weighty pleas for the internationalization of the seabed. International reactions to the Maltese proposals are examined by Guenter Weissberg, 18, *International and Comparative Law Quarterly* (1969), 41–102.

70. For the best-known general modern survey, see Douglas L. Oliver, *The Pacific Islands* (Rev. ed., Garden City, N.Y.: Doubleday; 1961). See also the instructive symposium, *Peoples and Cultures of the Pacific,* ed. Andrew P. Vayda (Garden City, N.Y.: Natural History Press, 1968).

71. See esp. Alan Moorehead, *The Fatal Impact* (London: Hamilton, 1966). See also W. P. Morrell, *Britain in the Pacific Islands* (London: Oxford University Press, 1960); Deryck Scarr, *Fragments of Empire* (Canberra: A.N.U. Press, 1967); and, for general studies of more recent political and other developments, John Wesley Coulter, *The Pacific Dependencies of the United States* (New York: Macmillan, 1957); Francis West, *Political Advancement in the South Pacific* (London: Oxford University Press, 1961).

72. Western New Guinea (West Irian) is under Indonesian administration; it was formerly a Dutch possession. New Guinea is a very large island, covering about 312,000 square miles.

73. Cf. Thomas R. Adam, *op. cit.,* X. In 1968 its budget was still under $1 million. Its headquarters are at Noumea in New Caledonia.

74. Adam, *op. cit.,* 129–132; K. O. Roberts-Wray, *Commonwealth and Colonial Law* (London: Stevens, 1966), 905–906.

75. See J. W. Davidson, *Samoa mo Samoa,* for a very full examination of Western Samoa in particular.

76. *Pacific Islands Monthly* (December 1967), 29. At first the Governor accepted this advice, but following the filing of a local law suit and a visit by him to Washington, he rescinded his decision, much to the annoyance of some of the chiefs.

77. See Norman Meller, *Study Mission to Eastern (American) Samoa,* a Report to the Senate Committee on Interior and Insular Affairs, 87th Congress, 1st Sess., 1961, by Senators Long and Gruening, Part III, 111–136. The population of Western Samoa is approximately 140,000 and that of American Samoa approximately 28,000. See further, Chap. VII, *post.*

78. For the accession of Tonga to a full measure of internal self-government, see the Treaty of Friendship of 1968 (U.K. Parliamentary

Papers, Cmnd. 3654(1968); Cmnd. 3921(1969).

79. See pp. 70–71, *ante*.

80. See pp. 165, 174, *post*.

81. On which see Robert Langdon, "Tahiti: Island of Love and Politics," *Pacific Islands Monthly* (June, 1968), 81. See also, more generally, *Le Monde* (Paris), September 22–23, 1968, p. 6, on unrest in the French overseas territories; and see also J. W. Davidson, "French Polynesia and the French Nuclear Tests," 2, *Journal of Pacific History*, (1967), 149.

82. There were disturbing manifestations of anti-Indian sentiment among indigenous Fijians in the late summer of 1968, when the Federation party, led by Indo-Fijians, captured all nine seats with increased majorities at by-elections held in the Indian communal constituencies.

83. See, for example, *Pacific Islands Monthly* (May 1968), 18–19.

84. The titles of recent American writings on the U.S. Pacific dependencies tend toward a certain uniformity, e.g., Robert Trumbull, *Paradise in Trust* (William Sloane Associates, 1959); Theodore F. Henning, *Buritis in Paradise* (Greenwich Book Publishers, 1961); Willard Price, *America's Paradise Lost* (John Day Co., 1966); Richard Barrett Lowe, *Problems in Paradise* (Pageant Press, 1967); David S. Boyer, "Micronesia: The Americanization of Eden," 132, *National Geographic Magazine* (1967), 702–744.

85. See, for example, J. T. Gunther, "Australia and Its Near Pacific Neighbours," *World Review*, Vol. 6, No. 1 (Brisbane, 1967), 3–16; W. E. H. Stanner, "British Pacific Island Territories and Papua–New Guinea," *Britain's Withdrawal from Asia—Its Implications for Australia* (mimeographed proceedings of a seminar convened by the Strategic and Defence Studies Centre [Canberra: A.N.U., September 29–30, 1967), 62–77; T. B. Millar, *Australia's Foreign Policy* (London: Angus & Robertson, 1968).

CHAPTER 6

For Forms of Government . . .

. . . . let fools contest;
Whate'er is best administered is best. . . .
(Alexander Pope)

He is his own greatest admirer. His has been
a life-long love story.
(Oscar Wilde)

I

SOME PROBLEMS OF SMALLNESS

Enough is known about problems of government and administration in those developing countries which are very small and relatively poor for a few generalizations to be offered: [1]

(1) Even if the territory forgoes or is denied the luxury of international diplomatic missions, the costs of government and administration tend to be inordinately high in relation to the size of the population. Expenditure on the salaries, official residences and cars of a Governor and his aides, or of Ministers, on a legislative building and legislative salaries, on administrative and police headquarters and the salaries of civil servants and police, on courthouses and judicial salaries, may be modest by the standards of large territories but still a heavy burden. Again, certain basic requirements for a reasonable standard of living in the modern age—e.g., pure water supplies, a sewage disposal system, electricity supplies, hospitals, adequate schools and roads—demand a high capital outlay, recurrent maintenance costs and the recruitment of experts and skilled technicians.

Sometimes they are provided with the aid of the administering power or of an international agency.[2] Too often, especially in small and remote islands, they are not provided at all. And, more generally, the economies of scale feasible in large units simply cannot be achieved.

(2) Because of low salaries, lack of social facilities and such luxuries as good libraries, and the dearth of opportunities for specialization or advancement, it is difficult for a small territory to recruit personnel necessary for efficient administration (e.g., competent accountants, economists, legal draftsmen and magistrates) and, if it recruits them, to retain them.[3]

(3) A visitor to a small island, even an island as populous as Mauritius, is constantly reminded that "everybody knows everybody else." Apart from providing material for titillating gossip, this may have a number of effects on government and administration. In the first place, considerations of social status, kinship, friendship, and personal background tend to matter more than individual merit when questions of leadership and promotion arise.[4] This is perhaps a very broad generalization, because even in communally divided or socially stratified societies like Mauritius and St. Kitts, men of humble origins (Ramgoolam and Bradshaw, for example) can rise to the top. But rigidity of social structure usually makes for inefficiency. Second, if deep political cleavages and animosities, based on community, ideology or personal faction, arise on a small island, the lot of those opposing the group in power is apt to be miserable. There may be no effective refuge, no place to hide, no alternative source of remunerative or prestigious solace. And it follows from this that the incentives to achieve political power and to cling on to it are all the greater. Third, particularly where the economy is narrowly based and the island poor, the activities of government are pervasive: government is the main employer; competition for good jobs in the public service is intense; accusations of nepotism and corruption abound. Fourth, it may be extremely difficult to find able persons with the requisite degree of impartiality,[5] or at least persons who are generally *accepted* as being impartial, to fill posts in which impartiality is of paramount importance. Politicians will often demand that senior and middle-grade civil servants and police officers be their active champions.[6] It will be hard to find independent-minded law officers, directors of audit, members of public service commissions,[7] even judicial personnel. Often

it may be desirable to have an independent Ombudsman. But if he is a local inhabitant he may fail to carry sufficient weight and be too vulnerable to political and social pressure to be really independent. In Mauritius, a not-so-small island governed in a liberal and tolerant way, it was generally agreed that there ought to be an Ombudsman, but that it was very important for him to be a non-Mauritian. More than four years have elapsed since agreement was reached on the principle, and an Ombudsman has not yet been attracted to the post. This points to a practical difficulty in implementing Dr. Benedict's interesting suggestion [8] that very small territories would do well to import a top administrator like the American town manager.

Some of these serious administrative problems can be reduced by functional cooperation between neighboring islands—a common court of appeal, a joint police force, a peripatetic Ombudsman. But these palliatives are feasible only where the will to cooperate is present.

II

THE IMITATION OF CONSTITUTIONAL FORMS

Administering countries have tended to reproduce their own constitutional features in their dependent territories. Their wards, after having served a prolonged and zealous pupilage, will in due course be admitted to membership of that select club which enjoys the full benefits of the metropolitan system of government. And the very fact of being denied some of these privileges, ostensibly on the ground that they are not ready to receive them, has stimulated among dependent peoples a clamant demand for the authentic article.

Britain lost the thirteen colonies largely because of a failure to understand that to grant to British settlers a representative legislature unaccompanied by a responsible executive branch of government was to court disaster. Belatedly the lesson was learned, and following the Durham Report responsible government with a parliamentary executive was introduced in the remaining North American colonies and in Australasia. It was only natural that India, after independence had been granted, should voluntarily choose the British system of executive-legislative relations in preference to any other. No former British dependency has adopted a system akin to the American, unless one points to Cyprus and Pakistan. But although those two countries, in their unique ways, adopted versions of the separation of powers doctrine, no student of the United States Constitution will recognize them as tributes to the American way of political life. Where substantial deviations from the Westminster model have taken place in Commonwealth countries after independence, they have usually been in the direction of vesting comprehensive powers, unimpeded by effective checks or balances, in the hands of an executive President.[9]

This is not to say that Westminster's export models have been replicas of the domestic product. The constitutions will be written; there will be special procedures for constitutional amendment, and judicial review of the constitutionality of legislation; there will normally be a justiciable bill of rights. None of these is a feature of the British Constitution. Executive-legislative relationships, regulated in Britain by unwritten convention and usage, will be partly defined in the constitution. There will be constitutional safeguards designed to secure the independence of the judiciary, and the impartiality of the civil service, the police, the conduct of elections, the audit of public accounts and the process of prosecution, different in form and often in substance from the corresponding rules and institutions obtaining in Britain. And there may be wide variations between one new constitution and another, devised to meet local pressures, demands and needs. The modern British approach has been a compound of principle and pragmatism.[10] Recently Zambia and Botswana became independent already equipped with an executive presidency. Malaysia, Lesotho and Swaziland have indigenous monarchs.

The American approach toward the constitutional evolution of its dependencies has been less flexible in one important respect—the separation of the executive from the legislature. That Micronesia at least needs to associate members of the legislature closely with the executive branch of government seems obvious to a British observer. But such a development is inhibited by doctrinaire attitudes in the United States Congress. In 1966, in the course of a hearing on a bill for giving the Virgin Islands an elected governor, it was proposed that the bill should be amended so as to explicity authorize the governor or his designated representative to attend meetings of the legislature and to speak there. This would be a restatement of an existing practice peculiar to that territory. Congressman Wayne Aspinall, the influential chairman of the House of Representatives Committee on Interior and Insular Affairs, opposed the amendment:

". . . what we are doing here is aborting the American system of government by bringing in a part of the so-called parliamentary practice. . . . What I object to is that we bring into our form of government something that is entirely foreign. . . ." [11] The amendment was withdrawn. The aberrant practice might continue informally but not with the seal of congressional approval. The rigidity of outlook displayed in the observations just quoted is quite remarkable. But, as one might have expected, some territorial politicians have themselves eulogised the separation of powers doctrine.[12]

American attitudes toward constitutional developments in the territories have not been hopelessly inflexible. There has been no dogmatic insistence on bicameralism. Nor do the territorial bills of rights confer a constitutional right to bear arms. In practice, moreover, the executive branch is almost invariably stronger vis-à-vis the legislature than on the mainland. Nor can it be said that a parliamentary executive along Westminster lines is necessarily the best pattern for very small developing countries. Under the British system the legislature is too often reduced to the status of a talking-shop or a rubber stamp. The government is usually assured of a permanent legislative majority and its legislative program will be duly enacted. The effectiveness of the ordinary legislator is seriously diminished by inability to secure the enactment of legislation disapproved of by the executive and in particular because of the rule which precludes passage of bills requiring the expenditure of government funds without the active support of the executive. In the Fiji Legislative Council every measure passed during the last decade has been a government bill.

Again, a very small legislative body may be overcrowded with office holders. In the House of Assembly in St. Kitts-Nevis-Anguilla in 1968 there were only two members of the Opposition, and one member on the Government side who held no office. In the British Virgin Islands, a Legislative Council of seven elected members, one nominated member and two ex-officio members, included a Chief Minister and two other Ministers who had to be appointed from among the elected members.[13] In such situations the Legislature lacks not only powers of initiative but also effective inquisitorial functions.

Some small territories present an anomaly of a different kind, not necessarily associated with a particular pattern of government. This is the inflated legislature. American Samoa has a Senate of eighteen members and a House of Representatives of twenty—one legislator for eight hundred inhabitants. Bermuda, with a population of some 50,000, has a House of Assembly of forty members and a nominated upper House of eleven members.[14] Antigua (60,000) also has a bicameral legislature, with ten senators, seven of whom are nominated by the Premier. There can be no hard and fast optimum size for a legislative body. A large assembly may be more closely in touch with the electorate, and in some political societies there may even be a case for enlargement through the exercise of a modicum of patronage. But unless (as in Jersey, for example) members are unpaid, and this may make it difficult for wage-earners to participate, the financial burden on a small territory will be heavy.

III

NEW EXPERIMENTS IN THE COMMONWEALTH

British official constitution-mongers have been uneasily aware for some time that institutiontal arrangements adapted from Britain may be unsuitable for very small territories. One possible answer to the problems may be a unification of executive and legislature in a single governing council.

This idea has been suggested partly by the precedent of the Channel Islands and partly by the British local government system. There are senior officials but no Ministers or indeed any identifiable political executive branch of government; policy and administrative decisions are taken by or under the authority or supervision of committees, and the most important figures in local politics are the chairmen of the main committees. Such a system can be cheap and flexible. It encourages the most constructive use of scarce resources of manpower. It may discourage artificial political divisions and deflate the pretensions of individual power-seekers.

An experiment broadly along these lines was carried out in Ceylon between 1931 and 1947. The chairmen of committees, however, were designated as Ministers and constituted as a Board, and the Governor retained broad powers. The experiment was not an unqualified success.[15] Lack of administrative coordination was its main defect, but in any event Ceylon, with its manifold political and communal divisions, was not the best of testing-grounds, and the Westminster model of cabinet government was introduced immediately before independence.

The general idea has nevertheless been resuscitated. In the Seychelles, a British colonial island group of some 50,000 inhabitants in the Indian Ocean, a single governing council, half of which is elected on the basis of universal suffrage, has been constituted.[16] In its legislative capacity the Council meets in public; in its "policy-making" and administrative capacity it normally meets in private. It is also divided into committees which exercise scrutinizing, supervisory and advisory functions with respect to specified areas of administration. The Governor retains wide discretionary powers. An integrated Governing Council has also been established in the Gilbert and Ellice Islands.[17] And in St. Helena (fewer than 5,000 inhabitants), although there remain separate Executive and Legislative Councils, both with an elected majority, a system of six committees of the Legislative Council, which may be entrusted with executive powers, has been set up, and the chairman of the committees are all members of the Executive Council.[18]

None of these territories has yet achieved full internal self-government; indeed, political advancement in the Gilbert and Ellice Islands has just begun. In each of them an appointed governor still wields important personal power. But in each of them elected members are associated with the executive branch of government without being designated Ministers; and this arrangement is not, apparently, conceived of as a halfway house to the Westminster cabinet system but as an arrangement intended to endure after the attainment of self-government. Such an arrangement will not be acceptable in every small British dependency; it was peremptorily dismissed by politically conscious people in the British Virgin Islands.[19] It will be appropriate only in those few places where local politicians are not particularly concerned about the indicia of ministerial status.[20] One notes that there are already two political parties in the Seychelles, and that external pressure for immediate decolonization is being brought to bear at the United Nations. The dual role of the Governing Council is incongruous: elected members, having agreed in private session on the merits of a government proposal, proceed to debate it in public session in their capacity as legislators. But the development of committees, even if their functions are circumscribed and the official element looms large, is better than inanition. And although the competent authorities in the United Statest know a great deal already about legislative committees, they may perhaps be moved by these experiments to think again about the sanctity of the separation between executive and legislature in their own dependencies.

The innovations outlined above do not, of course, offer any real guidance to solving problems of ultimate political status, except insofar as a territory which accommodates itself to a single council system is less likely to press hard for independence.

IV

THE UNITED STATES VIRGIN ISLANDS

In 1917 the United States purchased the Virgin Islands from Denmark (so as to ensure that Germany did not obtain a foothold in the Caribbean) for $25 million. Till 1931 they were under naval administration; since then they have been under the aegis of the Department of the Interior. The best short study of the Virgin Islands under American rule [21] was aptly entitled "Buying Trouble." But that was several years ago. In the 1960s the Virgin Islands have reached new frontiers and have glimpsed the great society. A beach-side plot on the idyllic island of St. John, bought for $50 in 1948, is said to have changed hands for $165,000 recently.[22] One wonders how many eyebrows were raised when the chairman of Discover America, a private promotional organization, declared that the islands were "distinctly fashioned by God for tourism." [23] Extravagant flights of euphoria by visitors are now commonplace.

The early years of American rule were punctuated by conflicts between a series of inept and uncomprehending governors and the separate councils (mainly elected, but on a narrow franchise) on St. Thomas and St. Croix. The economy languished, and the natives showed a disturbing lack of concern for the all-American virtue of self-help. From Congress little aid was forthcoming. But the Virgin Islanders received American citizenship by Congressional Acts of 1927 and 1932. The Roosevelt Administration secured the passage of an Organic Act in 1934, conferring almost universal franchise and constituting a single legislative assembly for the islands. The islanders were free to migrate to the mainland. The Federal Government and the appointed governor retained wide discretionary powers. Rivalry and antipathy between St. Thomas and St. Croix fragmented insular politics. Economic development was still slow. In 1954 the islands ceased to be a "possession" of the United States and became an "unincorporated territory." Further amendments to the Organic Act were made in 1960 and August 1968; the latter amendment made the office of governor elective as from 1970.

Meanwhile the economy had undergone a tremendous infusion of capital, particularly since the Kennedy administration and since the appointment of Ralph Paiewonsky, a white native of the islands and an accomplished fund-raiser and lobbyist, in 1961. The great leap forward was spurred on by massive federal development aid, much of it channeled through the Virgin Islands Corporation, a public body, accompanied by heavy private investment. The infrastructure of tourism was built and the sugar-based economy of St. Croix diversified. Today the islands have two jet airports and receive 750,000 visitors a year. St. Thomas is given over almost entirely to tourism, and an oil refinery and an aluminum plant have been built on St. Croix. Unspoiled St. John consists mainly of a national park presented by a member of the Rockefeller family. The islands receive federal grants on a more liberal scale than the states of the Union. Most of the excise duties collected in the United States on island products are refunded, though the islanders pay lower income tax rates. A mere 6% *ad valorem* duty is chargeable in the islands on foreign imports, and stateside tourists can purchase luxury goods there cheaply. Tax incentives are offered to outside investors. Special protection is accorded to the watch-making industry on St. Croix. As a result, the Virgin Islands enjoy a higher per capita income than several mainland states of the Union. The operating budget for the fiscal year beginning in 1968 was nearly fifty million dollars and the capital budget twelve and a half million dollars. The corresponding figures for nearby St. Kitts-Nevis-Anguilla, a territory with a slightly larger population (57,000), were barely one-tenth of these sums. These facts are worth recording because one would hardly expect radical politics to flourish in such an economic climate. Money can talk.

Up to now the Governor, the Government Secretary and the Government Comptroller have been federal appointees. Other government officials have been appointed locally, and this has given ample scope for patronage. In a recent hearing before the House of Representatives, the following dialogue occurred: [24]

"Mr. Morton: . . . Are there any non-Democrats in the Department of Public Works?
Mr. Henderson [Local Chairman of the Democratic Party and also the official responsible for hiring and firing P.W.D. personnel]: "If there are, I don't know of any."

Since then, tenure has been granted to many hitherto unclassified employees and the party activities of a wide range of officials curbed.

The Legislature is unicameral. In 1968 it consisted of fifteen senators elected biennially. All were engaged in business or the professions; nine were of African descent and one was a Puerto Rican. It sat for just over two months of the year, had eleven committees and was a remarkably productive body. In 1966 it passed no fewer than 295 bills. However, 41 of these were vetoed, some because they were of doubtful constitutionality, many because they allocated funds for purposes disapproved of by the Government, and a few because they made provisions for special advantages (e.g., licenses, leases, scholarships, jobs, paid leave) to particular individuals or groups. It is safe to assume that none of the bills thus vetoed would have been passed except on executive initiative in any British dependency where gubernatorial vetoes are rare because they are so seldom necessary.

This is not to say that executive-legislative relations in the American Virgin Islands were bad. On the contrary, 90% of Governor Paiewonsky's own legislative program was passed into law. In 1968 the Governor's majority faction of the Democratic Party (the Mortar and Pestle Democrats, or Unicrats) held nine seats in the legislature and the minority faction (the Donkey Democrats, unrecognized at the national level but strongly entrenched in St. Croix) held six. The Republican Party, saddled with blame for the years of neglect, had been in disfavor for many years.

As we have noted, the Executive is not rigorously segregated from the Legislature. The Governor not only addresses the Legislature at the opening of a session but holds legislative conferences and is sometimes invited to attend committees. And he sends a representative, usually the Director of Budget or the Attorney-General, to attend ordinary legislative sittings. But the Legislature remains a more effective body than its counterpart in any British dependent territory.

In the 1960s the problems of the American Virgin Islands have been social rather than political or economic. There are wealth and beauty on the islands, but a big gap lies between the rich and the poor. The cost of living is exceptionally high. Of the labor force, nearly a half is alien, drawn from neighboring English-speaking islands. Many of these immigrants live in typical Caribbean slums, one of the worst of which is adjacent to the run-down submarine base on St. Thomas. There has been a sharp increase in crime. And there are those who feel that the islands have been overdeveloped, socially and economically distorted and artificially Americanized.[25] Overdevelopment of its Caribbean dependencies is a reproach that Britain has yet to incur.

How do Virgin Islanders view their constitutional future? In 1965 a locally elected Constitutional Convention called for a number of reforms, including an elected governor, the abolition of the presidential veto over territorial legislation, a resident commissioner or delegate to the United States House of Representatives, and the right of the Islanders to vote in presidential elections. They sought on the one hand a larger measure of local autonomy, and on the other hand a closer identification with the United States. Legislation to provide for an elected governor had in fact been recommended to Congress by the Federal Government as early as 1959. Although the measure was substantially uncontroversial, it was not finally passed till 1968. For nine years Congressional committees and subcommittees dithered and procrastinated, conducting hearings, debating small amendments, and expatiating from time to time on the need for satisfying themselves that the Islanders were mature enough to be rewarded with a constitutional advance. This remarkable performance exasperated the Islanders ("Is the State of Mississippi mature enough to elect its own Governor?") and indeed the Federal Administration, as well. Had it not been for the fact that the Governor in office was generally regarded as the man most likely to have been elected, disenchantment in the Islands would have been more widespread. The United States is fortunate in having only five dependent territories on which to bestow the benefits of full self-government.[26]

One's impression is that Virgin Islanders envisage their ultimate status as being akin to the present Commonwealth status enjoyed by Puerto Rico. Statehood is regarded as an unrealistic goal because of the small size of the territory and the loss of economic advantages that full integration with the United States would involve. Independence would probably have even less support in the Virgin Islands than in Puerto Rico. The annual resolutions of the Committee of Twenty-Four calling for the implementation of Resolution 1514(XV) in the Islands are simply irrelevant, though some Islanders would like to see the Federal Government agree to receive a United Nations Visiting Mission so as to improve the education of outsiders with preconceived views.

The unexpected may, of course, happen. President Nixon's victory in November 1968 could have disturbing effects in the Islands unless they are tactfully handled. The replacement of Paiewonsky by an appointee from St. Croix on July 1969 was hardly an act of far-sighted statesmanship. Reactions to the disaffection of black militants on the mainland are not wholly lacking among the black Islanders. There could be a recrudescence of separatist sentiment in St. Thomas or St. Croix. Buoyant economies built on tourism have been known to founder. But at the present time the Islands see their future as lying with one another and with America. In his State of the Territory Message, delivered to the Seventh Legislature of the Virgin Islands on January 22, 1968, Governor Paiewonsky said:

> We are a part of the greatest Democracy in the world. While maintaining the burden of world leadership and responsibility, our country also evidences the greatest concern for the freedom of the individual and for his welfare. And that concern is not limited to America's shorelines. It extends from the jungles of Vietnam, where our young men are sacrificing themselves in this belief, to every other corner of the earth where hunger and disease remain and where our dollars and aid and volunteers are working. We are proud to be part of such a country and to share such humanitarian goals. . . . We are a part of America's future. . . .

These words rang strangely in the ears of at least one listener, to whom the American Virgin Islands seemed at least as much an American colony as (say) the Bahamas are a British colony. No governor or premier of the Bahamas would think of using similar language in relation to Britain. But then he remembered that, of course, the Virgin Islands were not an American colony.[27]

NOTES

1. See generally, on these matters, the valuable symposium *Problems of Smaller Territories,* ed. Burton Benedict (London: University of London, Athlone Press, for the Institute of Commonwealth Studies, 1967).

2. But the expert supplied by an international agency may be quite inexpert in dealing with a problem in a minuscule territory; see Geoffrey Burgess, "Administrative Development in Smaller Countries—the Capacity of Technical Assistance to Meet their Special Problems," 7, *Journal of Administration Overseas* (1968), 417–424.

3. Cf. Sir Arthur Lewis in Epilogue to Sir John Mordecai's *The West Indies: the Federal Negotiations* (London: George Allen & Unwin, 1968), 461.

4. See generally, Burton Benedict, "Sociological Aspects of Smallness," *op. cit.,* n. 1, *ante,* 45–55.

5. *Ibid.,* 8; D. P. J. Wood, *op. cit.,* 33–34. See generally, on the concept of impartiality, Thomas M. Franck, *The Structure of Impartiality* (New York: Macmillan, 1968).

6. A. N. Singham, "Legislative-Executive Relations in Smaller Territories," *op. cit.,* 137–139.

7. Cf. Sir Fred Phillips, 7, *Journal of Administration Overseas* (1968), 358–366. See also *Status and Problems of Very Small States and Territories* (Unitar Series No. 3, 1969), 162–180.

8. *Op. cit.,* 8–9.

9. The classic example is that of Ghana under Nkrumah. See F. A. R. Bennion, *Constitutional Law of Ghana* (London: Butterworth's 1962); Leslie Rubin & Pauli F. Murray, *Constitution and Government of Ghana* (2nd ed., London: Sweet & Maxwell, 1964). Ghana had become independent in 1957 under a Westminster-style constitution, which was what Nkrumah had striven for as far as executive-legislative relationships were concerned: see his *Africa Must Unite* (London: Heinemann, 1963), 66. This was superseded in 1960 by a republican constitution under which the President dominated both the Legislature and the Judiciary. Since the fall of Nkrumah in 1966 there has been a reaction in favor of a return to constitutionalism, and a liberal constitution was introduced in the summer of 1969.

10. See generally, de Smith, *The New Commonwealth and Its Constitutions* (London: Stevens, 1964); and the chapters on constitutional law in the *Annual Survey of Commonwealth Law,* ed. H. W. R. Wade (London: Butterworth's, 1965, 1966, 1967 and 1968).

11. Hearings on H.R. 11777 in the Subcommittee on Territorial and Insular Affairs, Washington, D.C., April 19, 1966 (Serial No. 89–27), 67, 68 (Congressman Wayne Aspinall).

12. See, for example, Gordon K. Lewis, *Puerto Rico* (New York: M. R. Press, 1963), 362–363.

13. See the Virgin Islands Constitution Order 1967, U.K. Statutory Instruments 1967 No. 1471.

14. U.K. Parliamentary Papers, Cmnd.3174(1967); U.K. Statutory Instruments 1968 No. 182.

15. See especially, S. Namasivayam, *The Legislatures of Ceylon* (London: Faber & Faber, 1951).

16. See the Seychelles Order, U.K. Statutory Instruments (1967) 5423. The introduction of the new constitution was based on a report by a Constitutional Commissioner in 1966, U.K. Parliamentary Papers, Commonwealth No. 1 (1967). At the time when the report was made, the composition of the Executive and Legislative Councils was already identical.

17. Gilbert and Ellice Islands Order, 1967, U.K. Statutory Instruments (1967), 3872. There is a Governing Council with executive and legislative powers and a House of Representatives with only advisory and consultative functions.

18. For the constitutional framework, see the St. Helena Constitution Order, 1966 (Statutory Instruments 1966, No. 1458).

For the local government arrangements in Pitcairn, the most minuscule of separate colonial dependencies see de Smith in *Annual Survey of Commonwealth Law* (1965) 36–37; *ibid.* (1966), 36–37. For a particularly good account of the island's history, see David Silverman, *Pitcairn Island* (Cleveland: World Publishing Co., 1967). Late in 1967 the island acquired its first mechanically propelled vehicle, and a few months later there occurred the first traffic accident.

19. See *Report of the Constitutional Commissioner,* Colonial No. 361(1965), §23.

20. In 1942 an authority described the Malays as "almost the least politically-minded people on earth" (Lennox A. Mills in Emerson, Mills & Thompson, *Government and Nationalism in South East Asia* [New York: Institute of Pacific Relations] 47). Malaya became independent in 1957.

21. Whitney D. Perkins, *Denial of Empire* (Leyden: Sythoff, 1962), V. For American rule between the Wars, see Luther N. Evans, *The Virgin Islands* (Ann Arbor: Edwards, 1945).

22. Carleton Mitchell, "Our Virgin Islands: 50 Years Under the Flag," 133, *National Geographic Magazine* 67 (1967), 86.

23. *San Juan Star* (Puerto Rico), January 28, 1968, p. 28.

24. Election of Virgin Islands Governor, Part I (Hearings before the Subcommittee on Territorial and Insular Affairs of the Committee on Interior and Insular Affairs, H. Rep., 90th Cong., 1st Sess., on H.R. 7330 and related Bills; Serial No. 90–15), June 17, 1967, p. 38.

25. An American statesider, working on St. Thomas, told me that he preferred Scarborough, in England, to Charlotte Amalie, the busy capital of the American Virgins. Scarborough is a relatively sedate seaside resort in Yorkshire, noted for bracing breezes and a dearth of sunshine.

26. Or four, if one regards Puerto Rico as having reached the stage where its constitutional destiny lies in its own hands.

27. Cf. Mary Proudfoot, *Britain and the United States in the Caribbean* (London: Faber & Faber, 1954). The Bahamas, though still a colony, have recently been restyled the Commonwealth of the Bahama Islands (U.K. Statutory Instruments 1969, No. 590).

CHAPTER 7

America's Pacific Dependencies: Unincorporated Territories

> . . . colonial establishments . . . [are] incompatible with the essential character of our institutions. . . .
>
> (John Quincy Adams)

I

ACQUISITION AND AFTER

The early phase of American expansion was continental. The west was won at the expense of the Indians and the French settlers. Louisiana was purchased and Florida acquired. The lands contiguous to Mexico were wrested in war. Alaska, bought from Russia in 1867, stood out as an exception. But at the end of the century it was joined by a motley group of other territories. The Hawaiian islands were annexed in 1898. In the same year Puerto Rico, the Philippines and Guam were taken from Spain in war. And in 1899 Samoa was partitioned between Germany and the United States. As we have noted, the Virgin Islands were purchased from Denmark in 1917, and a strategic trusteeship was established over Micronesia in 1947.

The Philippines achieved independence in 1946. The principle of independence had been accepted by the United States Congress in an Act passed in 1934, though implementation of the promise was deferred. Indeed, from the outset the American rule had generally been accepted as a passing phenomenon. The controversies about its termination—and they were very real and protracted—surrounded the timing and conditions of withdrawal.[1] In 1952 the territory of

Puerto Rico [2] became an internally self-governing Commonwealth. It seems likely that in the fullness of time its people will ask for statehood within the Union. In 1959 Hawaii and Alaska, after years of Congressional procrastination, were admitted as states of the Union. American Samoa acquired a fuller measure of self-government in 1967, and Guam and the Virgin Islands a still fuller measure in 1968, though these territories have not yet been regarded as serious candidates for statehood. Micronesia, indubitably a dependent territory, occupies, as we shall see, a unique position.

II

CONSTITUTIONAL CONSIDERATIONS

Under Article IV, Section 3, of the United States Constitution, Congress has power to dispose of and make all needful rules and regulations respecting the territory or other property belonging to the United States. This is the source of congressional authority over territories.

A judge-made distinction, now an accepted part of American jurisprudence,[3] was drawn at the beginning of this century between incorporated and unincorporated territories of the United States. An incorporated territory was an integral part of the United States to which the Constitution, with all its guarantees and prohibitions, applied, save insofar as the territorial government, unlike a state government, had no exclusive domain. "Incorporation," it has been said, "has always been a step, and an important one, leading to statehood." [4] This is historically correct—Hawaii and Alaska were the last two incorporated territories—though it would certainly not be correct to say that all territories which became states of the Union were regarded as being subject to the entire Constitution from the outset.

The concept of the unincorporated territory was devised ad hoc, in a manner immortalized by Mr. Dooley, to meet the problem of America's new insular possessions.[5] It was expounded with authority and a nicely calculated ambiguity by Mr. Justice White in *Downes* v. *Bidwell* (1901).[6] Its effect was to render the Constitution only partly applicable to these possessions, so that the guarantee of trial by jury, for example, was not implanted in an unreceptive soil. Certain express prohibitions in the Constitution and its amendments (for instance, the prohibition of bills of attainder and ex post facto laws) would extend to them automatically. How far other constitutional provisions would apply was to be deduced from congressional intent, the terms of the instrument of cession (if any) and the particular circumstances of the case.

At the present time, Guam, American Samoa and the Virgin Islands are unincorporated territories. The status of Puerto Rico is equivocal; probably it is in strict law an unincorporated territory, but Congress would not legislate for it without local concurrence on a matter of constitutional importance. Micronesia resembles an unincorporated territory. Like Guam, American Samoa and the Virgin Islands, its affairs are handled by the Office of Territories in the Department of the Interior, but it does not "belong" to the United States in the same sense. If one can draw a loose analogy with British constitutional law, American Samoa is comparable with a colony (which is technically part of Her Majesty's dominions) and Micronesia with a protectorate (which is not technically part of Her Majesty's dominions). The legislative and executive branches of the United Kingdom Government may enjoy the same plenary authority in a protectorate (e.g., the British Solomon Islands) as in a colony (e.g., the Gilbert and Ellice Islands).

A further distinction must be drawn between organized and unorganized territories. Thus, Guam and the Virgin Islands have Organic Acts, passed by Congress and alterable only by Congress, embodying their constitutions; American Samoa has no Organic Act, nor has Micronesia. This distinction has important practical implications. In the first place, the acquisition of an Organic Act has been regarded as a status symbol, a recognition by Congress that the local inhabitants ought to have a significant voice in ordering their own affairs. The alternative is constituent legislation by Executive or Secretarial Order. This could confer as full a measure of self-government as an Organic Act, and it may be (as with American Samoa in 1967) little more than a ratification of decisions taken by a locally elected Constitutional Convention. In practice, both in Washington and in the territories, organic legislation has been regarded as a reward for political maturity. And what Congress has granted, the Executive cannot take away. Second, proposed amendments to Organic Acts, even when given wholehearted support by the Department of the Interior, are likely to become bogged down for years in the morass of congressional committees and subcommittees. Members of the congressional committees on Interior and Insular Affairs are often well informed, sometimes ignorant; sometimes open-minded, sometimes dogmatic; often conscientious, sometimes overzealous; usually disinterested but sometimes narrowly partisan. And when an amending bill is reported out of committee, apathy, lethargy, a dogged devotion to measures dearer to the hearts of their constituents, mild opposition, or a minor disagreement between the two Houses, may result in the bill failing to pass into law till the next session, or the next, or the next. Constitutional change in British dependencies can normally be effected swiftly by executive legislation (almost invariably by the making of an Order in Council) without any parliamentary action. Parliamentary enabling legislation is required for the granting of independence or associated statehood, but not for advancement to internal self-government. Even an independence constitution will not nowadays be embodied in a bill subject to parliamentary amendment.[7] Third, the chronic congestion of Congress helps to explain why organized territories attach great importance to having Resident Commissioners in Washington and why governors frequently go to Washington to testify before committees. Fourth, the legal concept of an organized territory accounts more than any other factor for the absence of an Organic Act for American Samoa.

The present Constitution of American Samoa was approved by a Constitutional Convention and by a majority of the electorate in 1966, and ratified by the Secretary of the Interior under delegated powers; it came into force in July 1967. The main restrictions on autonomy may be briefly mentioned. The Governor and the Secretary of American Samoa are appointed in Washington, and the Governor is under the supervision of the Secretary of the Interior. He has a general constitutional power to make executive regulations not in conflict with existing laws. The Legislature must not legislate repugnantly to United States laws in force in American Samoa, or treaties or international agreements of the United States. It cannot appropriate funds other than those raised locally, though the Governor must submit a preliminary budget plan to the Legislature before transmitting to the Secretary of the Interior requests for federal funds. Bills are subject to the gubernatorial veto, which may be overridden by the Legislature after an interval of fourteen months, but the bill would then become law only with the approval of the Secretary of the Interior, whose approval is also required for locally proposed constitutional amendments. The Governor may veto items of appropriation bills, as well as having wide powers of appointment and removal of public officers.

More important, from the point of view of Congress, are certain peculiar features of the local Constitution and laws. There is a bill of rights, but there is no guarantee of the equal protection of the laws. On the contrary, Article 1, Section 3 of the Constitution provides:

> It shall be the policy of the Government of American Samoa to protect persons of Samoan ancestry against alienation of their lands and the destruction of the Samoan way of life and language, contrary to their best interests. Such legislation as may be necessary may be enacted to protect the lands, customs, culture, and traditional Samoan family organization of persons of Samoan ancestry, and to encourage business enterprises by such persons. No change in the law respecting the alienation or transfer of land or any interest therein, shall be effective unless the same be approved by two successive legislatures by a two thirds vote of the entire membership of each house and by the Governor.[8]

Protective discrimination, as it is known in American Samoa, is of doubtful constitutionality, and it is questionable whether Congress would be prepared to lend its ostensible authority to such arrangements. There may be similar objections to a grant of full American citizenship to the Samoans, inasmuch as the courts might conceivably read broad implications into the concept of citizenship. At present American Samoans are American nationals, with full freedom of migration to the mainland. The federal government has heavily subsidized their economy in the 1960s—federal appropriations reached a peak of thirteen million dollars for fiscal year 1963—and there has been a dramatic improvement in educational standards. But unless tourism develops on a grand scale, economic self-sufficiency (given modest natural resources, overcautious attitudes toward land-holding and a growing population) seems very far away. The disadvantages of union with Western Samoa are more apparent than any consequential advantages, and alternatives such as separate independence, or union with Hawaii, are even less attractive to the majority of American Samoans today. In the foreseeable future, the islands will remain within the American orbit. To put the matter conservatively, America must attach importance to denying the facilities of Pago-Pago to a hostile naval power. No doubt a fuller measure of internal self-government will be achieved during the next few years. But it is difficult to see how American Samoa will be fitted into any of the conventional categories, with the possible exception of free association in the style of Puerto Rico. Among the Samoans there has been little feeling of movement toward a determination of ultimate status.[9]

III

GUAM: WHERE AMERICA'S DAY BEGINS

"The people of Guam are without doubt among the most loyal Americans on the face of the earth." Perhaps the President of the Guam Junior Chamber of Commerce was carried away on a flight of hyperbole in the course of his testimony before a congressional subcommittee,[10] but perhaps he was not—for Guam is among the most improbable islands on the face of the earth.

Guam has been dominated by the West longer than any other Pacific territory. Discovered by Magellan in 1521, this island in the Marianas, 5,200 miles west of San Francisco, was annexed by Spain in the 1560s. The indigenous Chamorros were temporarily subjugated. A century later there began an organized mass conversion to Christianity. Native uprisings impeded the diffusion of the word of God. Military pacification restored the situation, and by the early eighteenth century spiritual enlightenment had been spread; but it is estimated that the Chamorro population in the Marianas had been reduced to barely one-twentieth of its former size in the process. The Chamorros have remained good Catholics ever since.

In the period of Spanish rule, subsistence agriculture was developed; little was done to disturb native institutions except insofar as they interfered with the purposes of the Church or of the administering power.

The United States acquired Guam at the same time as the

Philippines, using the island as a fueling station. It was placed under the Navy Department and governed by a procession of naval officers. In 1917 a nominated advisory Congress was created, becoming in 1931 an elected body, though still denied legislative powers. Congressional appropriations for Guam up to 1941 averaged thirty-five thousand dollars per annum. By that year the Guamanian population had grown to 22,000—an increase of 250%.

Under Japanese occupation the islanders suffered dire hardships. And there was fearful death and destruction when it was reconquered by the United States in the summer of 1944. Despite this the Guamanians celebrate Liberation Day on July 21 each year with great panache: beauty contests, firework displays, military parades and cock fights abound. This is possibly a light relief from the patriotic ardor of the Fourth of July, which is taken more seriously, perhaps, in Guam than anywhere on the mainland.

It is thought that some 200,000 American servicemen came to Guam in the last stages of the war against Japan. About 40% of the land—the island is just over 200 square miles in area—was preempted for military purposes. After the war the Guamanians, like the Maltese, were rewarded for their loyalty; Malta, having been awarded the George Cross for valor, was granted a substantial measure of self-government. The Congress of Guam was given legislative power in 1947 and the Guamanians received an Organic Act, full American citizenship and a civilian governor in 1950. A dynamic Guamanian, Manuel Guerrero, was appointed Governor in 1963. In 1968 the office of governor was made elective as from 1970. In 1969 Guerrero was replaced by Governor Camacho, also a Guamanian but more acceptable to the Nixon administration. For several years Guam has had an elected Resident Commissioner in Washington.

The life and economy of Guam are dominated by the presence of the American Navy and Air Force. The naval base is substantial, and has become an important haven for Polaris submarines; from the massive Andersen Airfield, B52s roar off to accomplish their missions in Vietnam. American military personnel and their dependants constitute some 30,000 temporary inhabitants, occupying at least two-thirds of the numbers in the island's telephone directory. The "indigenous" Guamanians, now an admixture of Chamorros,[11] Spaniards, Filipinos and other peoples, number about 38,000. Since there are also well over 10,000 resident Filipinos and statesiders, they have become a minority on their own island. The devastation of war and the needs of the armed services have transformed the economy. Agriculture has become unimportant. Guam has essentially a service and wage economy, and its relative prosperity is a by-product of heavy military expenditure. Between 1964 and 1968 more federal funds were allocated to Guam than in the period from 1898 to 1964. Were the Guamanians to call for the removal of the bases and for political independence (something which they have not experienced for over four hundred years), they would be requesting a calamitous decline in their present standard of living. Conscious of being overdependent on the needs of the armed forces, they hope to attract tourists from Japan and to entice industry. A Hilton Hotel and an oil refinery are under construction. The island has natural attractions, as well, despite its oppressively hot and humid climate. But the Guamanians cannot afford to bite the hand that feeds them. And they appreciate their good fortune in having a generous protector to aid them, for instance in the slow but architecturally successful reconstruction of Agaña, the capital, and in repairing the sixty million dollars' worth of damage caused by the typhoon of 1962 (which had reached a force of two hundred miles an hour).

To the casual visitor, the American way of life has indubitably made a big impact on the islanders. Agaña has American television programs, receives its news from American sources, has adopted the American educational system, sports neon lights, delicatessens and the noisiest discotheque in the Pacific. Affirmations of impassioned loyalty to the United States (including not infrequent references to the numbers of Guamanian volunteers and casualties in Vietnam) are commonplace. Whether these sentiments are superficial or not is irrelevant. Guam needs the United States, as Gibraltar needs Britain; and the United States needs Guam more than Britain needs Gibraltar. If a fundamental change in American policies were to take place—if the Navy were to leave, as it left Pago Pago in Samoa, or if the air base were to be phased out, causing heavy unemployment—Guamanian attitudes might change too. One recalls that in 1958 the Maltese Labor Party, having sought the political integration of Malta with the United Kingdom and having obtained British concurrence in principle, executed an abrupt about turn because of dissatisfaction with the British proposals for financial compensation to Malta as the naval installations on the island were reduced.[12] But possibly the case of Guam, ostensibly comparable to that of Malta, is to be distinguished on the ground that the sentimental attachment of Guam to America runs deeper. We may never know.

The only major clash between the Guamanian politicians and American federal authority during the last few years occurred in 1968 over the terms of the Elective Governor Bill. The Department of the Interior proposed—and it was supported in the United States congressional committees—that accompanying the grant of a wider measure of internal self-government there should be inserted into the Organic Act provision for a Government Comptroller in Guam, appointed by and responsible to the Secretary of the Interior, who would audit public expenditure and accounts. The Congress of Guam expostulated: they were being treated like a colony instead of a part of the United States; they were not being trusted; they were second-class citizens. In vain did the spokesman for the Interior Department explain that Guam was being dealt with in the same way as the Virgin Islands. The Guamanian Congressmen appealed to the American public by advertising their protest in *The New York Times* and *The Washington Post*. American Congressmen duly rebuked them for not having raised the money used for this purpose by public subscription. It seemed that the bill would founder yet again. But in the end it did become law.[13] Guam has to stomach the Government Comptroller. It has also had to stomach, for the time being, Governor Camacho.

Under the Organic Act, as now amended, there will be a popularly elected Governor and Lieutenant Governor. The Governor's legislative veto can be overridden by a two-thirds' majority of the Legislature, without further recourse to the Secretary of the Interior. As at present, the Congress of Guam will be unicameral, consisting of twenty-one legislators elected at large. Provisions of the Organic Act formerly giving preference in appointments and promotions in executive agencies to persons of Guamanian ancestry have been repealed. Further parts of the United States Constitution have been extended to Guam; and although Guam will still differ from a state of the Union in some respects (e.g., in its strict immigration controls, the rebate of federal taxes collected in Guam and on Guam-produced articles, the modification of American tariff laws, and the presence of an officer of the Department of the Interior to supervise government expenditure of federal imbursements instead of longer-range surveillance by the General Accounting Office), it will resemble a latter-day incorporated territory as much as an unincorporated territory. But formal incorporation has been resisted by the Department of the Interior because it implies a commitment to ultimate statehood.

The prospect of statehood has greater appeal in Guam than in the Virgin Islands, partly, perhaps, because Guamanians have a nagging fear of being cast adrift one day to subsist on their own meager resources; partly because they disclaim any sense of alienation from the American way of life; partly because they are aware of the enormous contrast between the prosperity of Hawaii, now a state of the Union, and most of the other Pacific islands. They would not welcome absorption by Hawaii,[14] with its more sophisticated and experienced businessmen. Some would welcome union between Guam and the other islands of the Marianas [15] which would offer only a modest increase in population, but one big enough to redress the ethnic imbalance and to provide outlets for local entrepreneurs, and perhaps to strengthen an ultimate claim to full integration with the United States. However, the other islands of the Marianas are a district of Micronesia, the Trust Territory of the Pacific Islands. The constitutional future of Guam cannot be shaped by the Guamanians alone. They are dependent on formidable external forces in this sphere as in so many others. When ex-Governor Guerrero declared, in a rare moment of infelicity, "We are America's doorstep," [16] he was uttering at least a half-truth.

NOTES

1. See further, Garel A. Grunder and William E. Livezey, *The Philippines and the United States* (University of Oklahoma Press, 1951); Whitney T. Perkins, *Denial of Empire* (Leyden: Sythoff, 1962), VI, VII.

2. See generally, Perkins, *op. cit.,* IV.

3. *Balzac* v. *Porto Rico* 258 U.S. 298, 305 (1922), per Taft, C. J.; though cf. doubts expressed in another context by Justice Black in *Reid* v. *Covert* 354 U.S. 1, 12, 14 (1957).

4. *Balzac's* case at 311.

5. See generally Perkins, *op. cit.,* I; Carl Brent Swisher, *American Con-*

stitutional Development (New York: Houghton Mifflin, 1943) XXI; Bernard Schwartz, *The Powers of Government* (New York: Macmillan, 1963), Vol. 2, 295–300.

6. 182 U.S. 244 (1901), 287–344; Frederic R. Couder, "The Evolution of the Doctrine of Territorial Incorporation," 26, *Columbia L. Rev.* (1926), 823–850.

7. See generally, K. O. Roberts-Wray, *Commonwealth & Colonial Law* (London: Stevens, 1966).

8. This repeats the terms of the corresponding provision in the Constitution of 1960. The Legislature is bicameral; the Senate is composed of eighteen matais (family heads) elected in accordance with Samoan custom by county councils, and the House of Representatives has twenty members (who need not be matais) elected on a basis of universal suffrage. These provisions appear to be constitutionally unobjectionable. In Western Samoa the franchise is still limited to matais; and in March 1969 the Western Samoan Parliament decisively rejected a proposal to introduce universal suffrage.

Till 1951 American Samoa was under naval rule. Only in 1960 did it acquire a legislature with law-making (as distinct from advisory) powers. For accounts of Samoan life and constitutional development, see Felix M. Keesing and Marie M. Keesing, *Elite Communication in Samoa* (Stanford University Press, 1956); John Wesley Coulter, *The Pacific Dependencies of the United States* (Macmillan, 1957); *Report of the Study Mission to Eastern American Samoa* (1961) (p. 91, n. 77, *ante*); Perkins, *op. cit.*, 269–299; Richard Barrett Lowe, *Problems in Paradise* (Pageant Press, 1967); and the Governor's Annual Report. This writer has not visited Samoa.

9. Cf. Ken McGregor in *Pacific Islands Monthly* (October 1968) 25, (November 1968) 60–67. However, legislation to set up a future Political Status Commission for American Samoa was adopted in 1969, presumably because of the precedent set by Micronesia.

10. Hearings before the Subcommittee on Territorial and Consular Affairs of the Committee on Interior and Insular Affairs (H. Rep. 90th Cong. 2nd Sess.) on H.R. 7329 and related bills (Serial 90–58) (January 24, 1968), 39.

11. Nowadays the term "Chamorro" normally refers to the language spoken by the Guamanians; it has many words traceable to Malay and Tagalog. Nearly all Guamanians also speak English, which is the medium of educational instruction.

12. Malta became an independent member of the Commonwealth in 1964.

13. Guam Elective Governor Act 1968 (Public Law 90–497), 90th Congress, September 11, 1968.

14. See Ruth G. Russell, *The United Nations and United States Security Policy* (Brookings Institution, 1968), 243–244, citing a recent controversy on the subject.

15. But in an unofficial plebiscite in November 1969, a majority of those voting disapproved merger with the Marianas. The turn-out was light (32 percent of registered voters).

16. As reported in the *Guam Daily News*, July 18, 1968, while requesting a congressional subcommittee for an increased appropriation for rehabilitation. The context was a reference to new local immigration laws designed to encourage Filipino immigration.

CHAPTER 8

Micronesia: The Background

. . . tiny pebbles, hidden in the bosom of the Pacific . . .

(Yanaihara)

I

In more than one sense the term "Micronesia" is a geographical expression, albeit ambiguous and imprecise. It can be used to denote those islands of the Pacific which are neither Polynesian nor Melanesian. For this purpose, Guam, Nauru, Banaba and the Gilberts are Micronesian islands; so are all the islands of the United States Trust Territory of the Pacific Islands, except the remote southern islets, Nukuoro and Kapingamarangi,[1] which are Polynesian. It can also be used to denote the entire Trust Territory, including its Polynesian outposts. For this purpose Micronesia excludes all other islands under separate administration.

In its broader meaning, Micronesia, the region of tiny islands, stretches over some five million square miles of the ocean, nearly all north of the Equator. Its total land area is minute—just over one thousand square miles. To the south and east lies Polynesia, the region of many islands. Farther southwest is Melanesia, the region of black islands. These names no longer represent culturally homogeneous entities, with the possible exception of Polynesia. They are convenient labels adopted as a means of rough classification. The diversity of ways of life in Melanesia, for instance, is very great. Saipan, Yap and Nauru, in Micronesia, differ from one another in many ways. For one untutored in social anthropology to attempt an analysis of the distinctive cultural characteristics of Micronesia would be an impertinence.[2] One can, however, point to certain features of social life apparent in most of the Micronesian islands: the household or extended family group, matrilineal succession, special kinship links, collective land tenure, small villages or hamlets, chiefly hierarchies, class systems, and so on. But great distances between small islands are inimical to conformity. And the impact of the modern overlords upon the islands has overlaid traditional patterns without establishing a new homogeneity. The Marianas have been significantly influenced by Spain and the United States, and to a small extent by Japan. Yap has, on the whole, clung to its own unique ways, though waves of intruders have broken over it. Palau adapted itself swiftly to the incursion first of Japan and then of the United States. Nauruans speak English with an Australian accent, having hitherto proved resistant to encroachments on traditional values.

The political entity now known as Micronesia, the Trust Territory of the Pacific Islands, consists of more than 2,100 islands, grouped in six administrative districts. The northern district is the Mariana Islands (excluding Guam). To the south, running approximately from west to east, are the four districts comprising the Caroline Islands (Palau, Yap, Truk and Ponape) and the Marshall Islands District. The sea area covered by the Territory is about three million square miles; its land area is barely seven hundred square miles. This is as if Mauritius had been burst into smithereens, the fragments flung about the Indian Ocean. By the end of 1969 the population of the Territory was approaching 100,000. At least nine distinct languages are spoken, apart from English and Japanese, two of them in the Yap District, three in the Ponape district, and one in each of the other districts.

It would be unwise to attribute ethnic characteristics to the Territory as a whole. That the biggest settlement of the islands in ancient times was the result of venturesome expeditions by Malay peoples, traveling vast distances in canoes, is probable. The present-day inhabitants of the Carolines are brown-skinned, fairly short of stature, and, to the outsider, not easily distinguishable from one another by reference to the islands from which they come. In the Marshalls there are traces of Polynesian characteristics. The indigenous Chamorros of the Marianas were said to be tall, and they may possibly have been of Polynesian origin. Today the people of the area are, on the whole, short, though tending to be markedly lighter-skinned than the people

TRUST TERRITORY OF THE PACIFIC ISLANDS
MICRONESIA

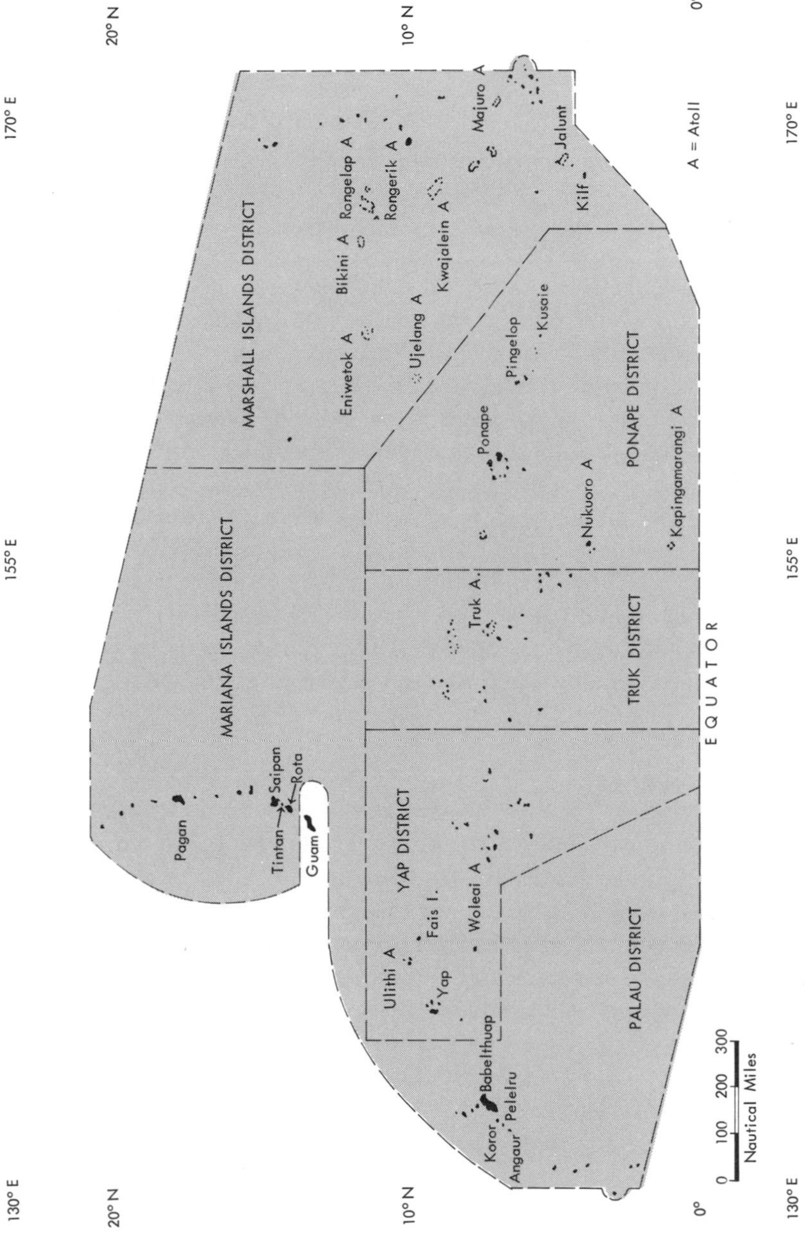

of other areas. The Japanese, during their administration, classified the "Chamorros" separately from "Kanakas" (other island peoples) in censuses.[3] Pigmentation and other physical characteristics have, of course, been affected by intermingling with Spaniards, other Europeans, Filipinos, Mexicans, Japanese and Polynesians, and to a small extent by interisland migration.

Geologically the islands fall into two main groups: the volcanic islands, protuberant peaks of a vast submerged mountain range; and the atolls, rings of tiny coral islets surrounding a lagoon. In the Marshalls, preeminently a region of atolls, there are over 1,150 separate islets;[4] the total land area of the district is only seventy square miles. The population of the Territory is concentrated on only ninety-six of the islands. But, given their vast dispersion and meager natural resources, the problem of providing adequate services is immense.

Climatic variations in the Territory are not large. The islands are tropical and generally humid, and (though periods of drought are not unknown) annual rainfall is heavy; in Ponape it sometimes exceeds three hundred inches in a year. Mean temperatures differ little from month to month. The day is hot, night scarcely less warm. Most of the islands lie in the shadow of an unpredictable menace—the typhoon. In recent years the Marianas have suffered the brunt of the most ferocious typhoons. Having observed the after-effects of such a catastrophe on one of the larger and higher islands, the writer does not find it hard to imagine how cataclysmic must be the impact on a low-lying atoll or an isolated islet in the Carolines[5] or the Marshalls.[6]

II

The recorded history of the islands now forming the Trust Territory is complex. We have already mentioned the discovery and annexation of the Marianas[7] by Spain in the sixteenth century. For the purpose of better subduing and enlightening the rebellious natives, the Spanish administration had the survivors removed from the Northern Marianas (Saipan, Rota, Tinian and Pagan were the principal islands) to Guam at the end of the seventeenth century. Control of movement was relaxed after order had been restored, but at the commencement of German rule two hundred years later the native population of the Marianas other than Guam was still under 2,000.[8] Today it is in the region of 11,000. Early estimates that the islands supported a substantially higher population before the coming of Spain are not implausible.

In 1686 a Spanish explorer discovered a group of islands farther south and named them the Carolines; this name was later given to islands extending over a wider area. The Spanish missionaries who hastened to the area found their proselytizing zeal unrewarding. Spain, however, purported to exert a shadowy suzerainty over the area.

From the 1780s, new visitors began to arrive in the scattered southern isles of Micronesia. British navigators named the Gilberts and the Marshalls, and rediscovered Palau. There followed the whalers from New England and Britain, who, when they were not engaged in their peculiarly hazardous occupation, introduced the natives to the most pernicious by-products of western civilization. German traders in copra and other commodities established themselves in the Marshalls and the Carolines. O'Keefe, the most celebrated of maritime traders, built up his private kingdom on Yap. American Protestant missionaries, in the face of opposition from whalers and traders, came to spread the gospel among the heathen, and met with a fair measure of success; they were particularly successful in inducing the natives to clothe themselves, less successful in imparting the virtues of chastity. There were occasional visits by American, Russian, British, French and other warships, sometimes to exact retribution, indemnities or undertakings for wrongs done to the nationals of their own countries. The British distinguished themselves by executing a high chief of Palau and razing a Palauan village; the latter venture was a reprisal for failure to pay compensation for the alleged plundering of a ship belonging to the renowned O'Keefe.

Not till the 1870s, the beginning of the golden age of imperialist expansion, did international political rivalry become a significant factor in Micronesia. Spain, irritated by the growth of German trade in the Carolines, claimed the right, as an absentee sovereign, to impose restrictions on foreign commerce. In 1885 Spanish warships were despatched to occupy Yap, but found themselves narrowly forestalled by German marines, who proclaimed in Yap and on other islands the sovereignty of the Fatherland over the Carolines. The dispute was referred to Pope Leo XIII, who made an award in favor of Spain, subject to the maintenance by Spain of orderly government in the islands, freedom of trade and settlement for Germans, and the right of the German Navy to use ports of call.

The subsequent attempt by Spain to administer its domain in the Carolines was disastrous. For Spain the primary purpose of government appeared to be the expulsion of Protestant missionaries and the elimination of Protestantism. The upshot was a series of local revolts accompanied by bloodshed and repression, terminated only upon the purchase of the Carolines (together with the Marianas other than Guam) by Germany in 1899. With the United States' appropriation of Guam and the Philippines as the spoils of war, Spain ceased to be a colonial power in the Pacific. But Germany was now in the picture. Already installed in the Marshalls (where its authority had been accepted since 1885), New Guinea and Nauru, it arranged to partition Samoa with the United States, obtaining the lion's share. Coupled with its new Micronesian acquisitions, Germany's holdings were more extensive than those of any other European power in the South Seas.

The German period of administration in Micronesia was brief, moderately competent, and uneventful. It was brief inasmuch as it ended in 1914. Law and order were maintained, often by harsh and peremptory methods (as when an uprising occurred in Ponape), by natives recruited from other islands under the command of German officers. There were little more than twenty resident civil administrators. Religious toleration was introduced. The Germans were moved not by liberal impulses—the paramount duty of the natives was obedience—but by a desire for another place in the sun, where trade and communications could be conducted under the most appropriate auspices, which happened to be those of the Reich. A cable and radio station was established on Yap, and the natives were required to build roads there. Phosphate deposits were discovered, and swiftly exploited by the use of forced labor, on Angaur Island in the Palaus. Carolinian emigration to the depressed and depopulated Marianas was encouraged and, in some instances, made obligatory.

But the eyes of the Japanese were already turning southward. Japanese commercial penetration of the Marianas and the Carolines did not begin till the 1890s, but within a few years Japanese firms were ousting the German companies from their dominant position in the copra trade, and soon they took to developing fishery enterprises and the collection of mother-of-pearl. By the time war broke out in 1914, a northern sun had risen over Micronesia.[9]

III

In October 1914 the Japanese Navy seized the German islands north of the equator. The legitimacy of the occupation was covertly recognized by Britain and then the other principal European allied powers, and at the Versailles Conference Japan sought outright annexation of the Marianas, the Carolines and the Marshalls. But Wilsonian principles prevailed and Japan had to be content with a "C" Mandate over the islands. For practical purposes this was a distinction without a difference: the islands became a Japanese colony.

Under the Mandate, which came into force in 1930, Japan undertook to "promote to the utmost the material and moral well-being and social progress of the inhabitants of the territory." Slavery, forced labor and the sale of alcohol to natives were to be prohibited. There was to be freedom of religion. The islands were not to be used for military purposes. And there were other obligations cast on the Mandatory. But the territory could be administered as if it were an integral part of the Mandatory's own dominions.

That Japan ignored the prohibition on the establishment of bases,[10] and indeed used Truk in the Carolines as its main southern jumping-off ground for the grand assault in December 1941, is well known. To a large extent it was successful in veiling its activities, virtually excluding foreign commerce, severely curtailing entry of foreign missionaries, and placing multitudinous administrative difficulties in the way of prospective visitors from abroad.[11]

A judgment of the Japanese regime in Micronesia cannot be wholly adverse when comparisons are drawn with the other recipients of "C" Mandates. For the first, and one is obliged to say the only, time a serious attempt was made to develop the economic resources of the region. But this development took place not only under Japanese auspices and with Japanese private capital but also with Japanese labor. By 1940 some 70,000 Japanese, Okinawans and Koreans, most of them regular settlers, had emigrated to the islands. In the years between, the native population had shown only a slight increase, to about 50,000, and was thus outnumbered by the settlers. Native labor was employed in the exploitation of phosphates and later bauxite, in the copra industry, and in the construction of public works. Some Micronesians also found employment as minor functionaries, teachers, technicians and domestic servants. However, the major undertakings introduced by the Japanese—the production of sugar and alcohol in the Marianas, fisheries in Palau, Ponape and Truk, steamship and air communications, the keeping of livestock—and minor innovations such as coffee and pineapple farming, good restaurants, motion picture theaters, beauty parlors and geisha houses were conducted exclusively by the Japanese themselves. To a very large extent the role of the Micronesian natives in the new scheme of things was irrelevant. If they had disappeared altogether, doubtless new Japanese and Okinawan immigrants would have come in to take their places.

In retrospect one can say that for Japan the mandated area served three purposes: it was a potential strategic asset; it provided a minor outlet for the country's surplus population; it was a source of supply for certain primary products (notably sugar and phosphates) which Japan needed. Taken as a whole, the territory was not a significant economic asset: till 1932 it received grants in aid from the home government, and the main sources of internal revenue were duties on sugar and phosphates borne by Japanese domestic consumers; the profits earned by the Japanese companies controlling the local economy or exporting consumer goods there were welcome to the shareholders, but the part played by the islands in the Japanese economy as a whole was extremely small.[12]

The islands were governed, after the first years of naval rule, by the South Seas Administration (*Nanyo-cho*). In 1935 this Administration had over nine-hundred Japanese employees and the number was still increasing. The Japanese were infinitely more thorough and painstaking than their German predecessors. The seat of government was Koror in Palau; this became a flourishing metropolis. (So, indeed, did Garapan in Saipan.) The system of government was both bureaucratic and autocratic. Laws were made for the territory by imperial ordinances and Governors' orders. The instruments of native administration were village chiefs and headmen. This relationship could be regarded as a form of indirect rule only insofar as the Japanese appointees were the same persons as the traditional rulers, and often they were not. In any event, no appreciable field of autonomy was left to these indigenous leaders.

Under the Japanese the old hierarchical structure of Micronesian society began to disintegrate. The Micronesians were introduced to a monetary economy, new tastes and a more sophisticated civilization. They parted with much of their land by sale or lease for exploitation by the newcomers. Basically, though, they were peripheral to this self-sufficient new order. It is misleading to assert that it was the policy of the administering authority to Japanize the natives as quickly as possible.[13] Certainly they were taught the virtues of obedience to new rulers and were subjected to official propaganda. They were encouraged to send their children to public schools for a course of study lasting two or three years, most of which consisted of instruction in the Japanese language (though Japanese children in the territory went to separate schools). Selected notables were despatched to Japan for special visits. And there was a good deal of intermarriage with Japanese immigrants, but this implied tolerance rather than official encouragement. The Micronesians were onlookers, participating but little in the imported economy and not at all in the formation of policy. It is fair to mention that the Japanese administration did something to improve standards of public health among the natives, and that the decline in population, save in Yap, was arrested. But the sums devoted by the Government to the direct promotion of native social welfare were trifling. In these respects the Japanese were no worse than most of the other administering powers in the Pacific.[14]

As war grew near, the Japanese regime became dominated by the military authorities. The Micronesians were subjected to an increase in forced labor and the requisitioning of more land for military purposes. The big influx of Japanese servicemen depressed the importance of the Micronesians in the life of their own islands to a still lower level. With the advent of American naval supremacy, supplies to the islanders were reduced. Outlying islands not being used for military purposes were left to their own resources. In 1944 the islanders were exposed to the harshest blows of war—bombing, naval bombardment, and eventually reconquest by land, in some instances (notably Saipan in the Marianas and Peleliu in the Palaus) in the face of desperate Japanese opposition. Perhaps as many as three or four thousand Micronesians died in the course of or as a result of these operations. The number will never be known, but it is certain that destruction of property was very heavy. Japanese casualties were massive.

IV

During the last year of the war the islands served as an assembly area and an advanced American air and naval base for the final assault on Japan. New runways were constructed among the sugar plantations of the Marianas. The Micronesians experienced a new occupation, more overwhelming in numbers but on the whole more benign than any of its predecessors. Japanese administration was superseded by American military government under the Commander in Chief of the Pacific Forces in Hawaii.

These conditions must have stretched the American aptitude for improvisation. The difficulties were enhanced by rapid demobilization, which was accompanied by the compulsory repatriation of all Japanese civilians to their homeland. By the early part of 1946 the problems were almost overwhelming. Much of the land area of Micronesia had been devastated by war or taken over for airfields and other military installations which had quickly fallen into disuse or were being dismantled. The islanders were losing their new source of temporary employment and the Japanese, the mainstays of the economy, were gone. Gone too, were many dwellings, nearly all savings, a wide range of consumer goods and regular means of transportation. The cultivation of copra and other crops had already suffered by the economic distortion during the war years and from the depredations of pests. The task of rehabilitation would have been colossal even were it given high priority. It was not. Useful preliminary work was done by the United States Commercial Company, working as an agent of the Navy, but personal relations between the Company's economic specialists and the naval administrators became so bad that the Company had to be wound up after a brief life. It would be neither feasible nor relevant to evaluate the competence of naval administration.[15] Certainly after 1946 it was strengthened by a corps of university-trained specialists in civil administration. But one can safely assert that twenty years later, long after naval administrators had given way to civilians, large areas of Micronesia had not been restored to the prewar standard of living under the Japanese.

While harassed administrators in the islands were wrestling with insuperable problems, two decisions were made within the United States Government. The United States would propose at the United Nations that it assume a strategic trusteeship over the islands, and the islands would be placed under the Department of the Navy and not the Department of the Interior: both highly controversial decisions at the time.[16] The concept of strategic trusteeship appeared to be de facto annexation, papered over with the thinnest of disguises.

On the other hand, trusteeship implied a measure of international accountability, and as such was initially resisted by American advocates of outright annexation. In any event the trusteeship agreement was submitted to the United Nations on February 26, 1947, and was approved with ostensibly minor amendments by the Security Council on April 2. The Soviet Union, which had voted against the eight trusteeship agreements already adopted by the General Assembly, cast its vote in the Security Council in favor of the agreement for the Trust Territory of the Pacific Islands.[17]

NOTES

1. For a lively description of life on these islets, see E. J. Kahn, Jr., *A Reporter in Micronesia* (New York: W. W. Norton, 1966), XVI–XIX.

2. Cf. Leonard Mason, "The Ethnology of Micronesia," in *Peoples and Cultures of the Pacific,* ed. Andrew P. Vayda (Natural History Press, 1968), XV for a good short survey with a useful bibliography. See also Douglas L. Oliver, *The Pacific Islands,* VI.

3. Tadao Yanaihara, *Pacific Islands under Japanese Mandate* (New York: Oxford University Press, 1940), 30; this classification was adopted for all administrative districts. Yanaihara mentions that the Kanakas were particularly despised for their aversion to hard work (7).

4. All the present district centers except Majuro in the Marshalls are located on relatively high islands.

5. Cf. John Wesley Coulter, *The Pacific Dependencies of the United States* (New York: Macmillan, 1957), 164; William A. Less on Ulithi in the Yap Islands District in *Peoples and Cultures of the Pacific,* 330–379.

6. Coulter, *op. cit.,* 293, 294.

7. They were thus named in 1668.

8. Yanaihara, *op. cit.,* 41.

9. Cf. Yanaihara, *op. cit.,* 23–28.

10. But it seems that large-scale militarization of the territory was not introduced till the late 1930s: Richard Dean Burns, "Inspection of the Mandates, 1919–41," 37, *Pacific Historical Review* (1968), 445–462.

11. Cf. Willard Price, *America's Paradise Lost* (John Day Co., 1966). The United States recognised Japanese rights in Micronesia in 1922, and was given an assurance that it would be entitled to make use of the communications facilities on Yap; these facilities were never in fact accorded.

12. Cf. Yanaihara, *op. cit.,* IV.

13. Coulter, *op. cit.,* 173.

14. The main source of factual information about Japanese rule up to 1935 is Yanaihara's *Pacific Islands under Japanese Mandate.* Although the book was published in 1940, no reference whatsoever is made to the militarization of the islands (see, however, Burns, *loc. cit.,* note 10, *ante*). Shorter and more critical accounts appear in a number of other works. See, for example, Oliver, *op. cit.,* XVIII; Kahn, *op. cit.,* II.

15. For a useful short account of the first three years of American administration, see Roy E. James, Rupert Emerson and others in *American Pacific Dependencies* (New York: American Institute of Pacific Relations, 1949), VIII.

16. For the debate within the United States Government over the question of trusteeship extending back into the war years, see Ruth B. Russell and J. Muther, *A History of the United Nations Charter* (Brookings Institution, 1958), 336–346, 573–587.

17. See Emerson, *op. cit. supra,* 22, quoting Mr. Gromyko's words which expressed unqualified approval of the general principle underlying the agreement.

CHAPTER 9

Micronesia: In Trust

. . . this seat of Mars,
This other Eden, demi-paradise . . .
This happy breed of men, this little world . . .
. . . bound in with the triumphant sea.
(William Shakespeare, *Richard II*)

"That is well said," replied Candide, "but we must cultivate our garden."
(François M. A. de Voltaire, *Candide*)

I

The trusteeship agreement,[1] having been approved by the Security Council on April 2, 1947, was submitted to the United States Congress. On July 18, 1947, Congress passed a Joint Resolution [2] authorizing the President to approve the agreement on behalf of the United States. Presidential approval was given at once. The agreement came into force that day. Plenary legislative and executive authority was assumed to be vested in the President, and was exercised by him from time to time in Executive Orders. In 1954 the exercise of this authority was placed on a more secure statutory foundation.[3] The constitutional framework of the territory is now embodied in a series of Secretarial Orders made under full powers delegated to the Secretary of the Interior by the President.[4] The framework must, of course, be viewed against the background of the trusteeship agreement.

Under the agreement, the Administering Authority has (subject to the agreement) full powers of administration, legislation and jurisdiction over the territory [5] and may apply to the territory the laws of the United States in its discretion. The entire territory is designated a strategic area, permissible under Article 82 of the U.N. Charter. In accordance with Article 83 of the Charter, the Security Council is responsible not only for the approval of the Agreement and (through the Trusteeship Council) the supervision of its implementation, but also for making any decisions on alteration or amendment. By necessary implication, termination of the agreement must also require the concurrence of the Security Council. Decisions of the Security Council in these matters are subject to veto by the permanent members. The agreement itself specifies (Art. 15) that, alteration, amendment or termination is possible only with the consent of the Administering Authority. The prospects of ultimate deadlock are not uninteresting.

Most of the other terms of the agreement follow closely the wording of the Charter. According to Articles 76a and 84 of the Charter, a basic objective of the trusteeship system is the furtherance of international peace and security. The administering authority is therefore permitted by the Agreement (Art. 5) to establish bases, erect fortifications, and station and employ armed forces in the territory, as well as using for defense local volunteer forces. The United States has not raised a Micronesian armed force. Its interpretation of authority to employ its armed forces in the territory has, however, extended to the conduct of nuclear tests. Under Article 13 of the agreement the Administering Authority may also close areas for security reasons without detailed scrutiny by the Trusteeship Council.

According to Article 76b of the Charter, the Administering Authority is to promote the advancement of the local inhabitants and their "progressive development towards self-government or independence as may be appropriate to the particular circumstances of each territory and its peoples and the freely expressed wishes of the peoples concerned. . . ." Article 6 of the Agreement substantially reproduces this wording, with some embroidery. The reference to independence was inserted into the agreement as a result of an amendment introduced by the Soviet Union. The United States representative, accepting the amendment, nevertheless expressed the view that the unexceptionable principle of independence could not be realized in the territory within the foreseeable future.

Article 76c of the Charter enjoins respect for human rights. Article 7 of the agreement provides for an absolute guarantee of freedom of conscience and qualified guarantees of freedom of speech, the press, assembly, worship, religious teaching, migration and movement. The Code of the Trust Territory does in fact embody a wide-ranging bill of rights, including freedom to petition, the prohibition of slavery, protection against unreasonable search and seizure, due process of law, the prohibition of ex post facto laws and of excessive bail, excessive fines and cruel and unusual punishments, freedom from discrimination, the right of free elementary education, no imprisonment for debt, and due recognition of local customs; there is no guaranteed right to bear arms.

Article 76d of the Charter states the objective of equality of treatment in social, economic and commercial matters and in the administration of justice for nationals of other United Nations members, subject to the provisions of individual trusteeship agreements. Article 8 of the agreement modifies the application of this general objective by placing nationals and associations of the Administering Authority in a more favored economic position than those from other members, and giving the Administering Authority control over flying rights in the territory. The door was not open; it was left barely ajar.

Among other terms of the agreement, the most intriguing is Article 9, empowering the Administering Authority to constitute the territory into a customs, fiscal or administrative union or federation with other territories under United States jurisdiction "where such measures are not inconsistent with the basic objectives of the international trusteeship system and with the terms of this agreement." Any attempt to activate this long-ignored option today, or to terminate the trusteeship agreement by uniting the territory politically with Hawaii or Guam, would certainly arouse strong opposition at the United Nations.

II

The first fifteen years of American administration in the trust territory excite no enthusiasm and little admiration. True, the problems of administration were immense. In the first place, the Japanese settler economy lay shattered, for the settlers had been deported. The sugar plantations lay waste. Deep-sea fishing was almost entirely abandoned. Fish canning and drying industries collapsed. Pearl cultivation disappeared. The phosphate deposits were soon exhausted. Livestock was depleted. Even copra production languished, partly because of the depredations of the rhinocerous beetle. The disappearance of the naval base from Dublon on Truk and the administrative headquarters from Palau, and the reduction of Garapan—to this very day a wretched, straggling village—to rubble eliminated major sources of local employment. In fact the Micronesians experienced a sharp reduction in their standards of living—a reduction rendered all the more acute by improvements in public health leading to overpopulation in some areas: the median age of the population today is fifteen.

Second, the devastation caused by war demanded a comprehensive rehabilitation plan, vigorously executed, to reconstruct dwellings, remove debris and reestablish the foundations of a viable economic order. Supply failed to meet the demand.

Third, there were the ineluctable problems presented by a scatter of widely dispersed small islands. Not only is it impracticable to achieve economies of scale; not only is the cost of administration inordinately expensive if adequate services are to be provided for all; the maintenance of reasonable communications for the elementary purposes of administrative coordination and supervision is extremely difficult. For instance, from Koror, the district headquarters in Palau, to Majuro, the district headquarters in the Marshalls, the distance is well over 2,000 miles as the crow flies, and the crow did not fly. Even today, now that regular and fast air services are available, the distance between these two centers via Saipan, the territorial headquarters, is 2,709 miles. It is worth mentioning that only seven or eight of the islands have a population of over 3,000, and that the large majority of inhabited islands are atolls with fewer than five hundred inhabitants.

Fourth, the United States had no experienced corps of "colonial" administrators.[6] Recruitment of suitable personnel was difficult, except at the higher levels, and those who came to the territory were prone to depart too soon.

Confronted with these problems, what did the United States do for the territory? Down to 1962 the answer was precious little, with one major and incongruous exception. That exception was Saipan in the Marianas, where the Navy held sway (apart from a brief period from 1951 to 1953). A substantial complex of buildings, roads and other facilities was constructed at a reputed cost of twenty-eight million dollars, in the interior of the island, away from prying eyes. But the main object of this impressive exercise was not to house the territorial administration—the seat of government at that time was outside Micronesia—but to provide a training ground for Chinese Nationalists under CIA instruction, in preparation for the grand assault on the mainland.[7] This absurd enterprise has had some significant by-products: the provision of adequate accommodation for the territorial government headquarters when it did move to Saipan in 1962; a distortion of the economy of Saipan away from agriculture and toward wage earning in public service; an assimilation of attitudes in Saipan to those in Guam; and the encouragement of separatist tendencies in Saipan, not least because of its superior standard of living compared with other islanders in the Trust Territory.

Other defense activities, more formidable and more destructive, were carried out in the northern atolls of the Marshall Islands. In 1946, before the trusteeship agreement was operative, the 167 inhabitants of Bikini atoll were removed to Kili, a tiny single island without a lagoon in the far south of the Marshalls. (Originally they had been sent to nearby Rongerik, but the vegetation and fish there were apparently blighted by an ancient curse.[8]) Bikini was duly blasted by nuclear explosions; the Bikinians pined away on Kili. Not until 1968 was it possible to begin preparations for their return to their stricken home.[9] In 1948 the 137 inhabitants of Eniwetok were evacuated to Ujelong atoll, which has a land area of only one-third square mile. There they remain, protesting from time to time the food shortages. Eniwetok still plays its mysterious part in the maintenance of international security. In 1954 a hydrogen bomb test in the Bikini lagoon area inflicted radioactive fall-out damage on the people of Rongelap atoll. Eleven years passed before the United States Congress appropriated funds for compensation.[10] Financial reparation to the involuntary evacuees of Bikini and Eniwetok had been made more promptly. At the present time the only major strategic activity known to be carried on in the territory is the anti-missile missile testing station of Kwajalein, also in the Marshalls. A large community of Micronesian laborers, attracted by the high wages paid by the service authorities on Kwajalein, has crowded on to the minute island of Ebeye close by.[11] Curiously enough, the Marshallese are widely reputed to be more pro-American than the people of any district in the territory, with the exception of the Marianas.

From this digression one can return to potted constitutional history. In 1951 the period of naval administration, distinguished mainly by the encouragement of some valuable anthropological surveys, ended and responsibility for the administration of the Territory was relinquished to the Department of the Interior. In 1953 the Marianas other than Rota were returned to the Navy, responsibility for the district being allocated to the Commander in Chief of the United States Pacific Fleet in Hawaii and delegated by him to the Commander of the Naval Forces in Guam. A High Commissioner for the Territory had been appointed in 1951, but down to 1954 he too had his headquarters in Honolulu; in the latter year he moved closer to his diocese, but remained just outside it in Guam. In 1962 the Navy relinquished the Saipan District. The Interior took over, and the High Commissioner at last moved into Capitol Hill on Saipan.

Meanwhile attempts were being made to develop local representative institutions. From 1956 onwards municipalities were established in most parts of the territory. (The non-American reader must be told that a "municipality" is often a collection of villages and hamlets.) In 1959 district congresses, partly or wholly elected, were first constituted. A nominated interdistrict advisory council, meeting in Guam for a week each year, was set up in 1956; this became a directly elected body (with a member from Saipan), the Council of Micronesia, in 1961, and was the direct forerunner of the Congress of Micronesia.[12]

Till 1961 the territory was not subjected to close scrutiny by the United Nations. Visiting missions appointed by the Trusteeship Council dallied but briefly in Micronesia; they had other trust territories in the Pacific to visit. But with the announcement of Western Samoa's forthcoming independence, and the swift surge to independence among the African trust territories, it became feasible for visiting missions to conduct proper surveys of individual Pacific territories. The 1961 Mission[13] spent several weeks in Micronesia. Its report was not hypercritical, but pointed to so many deficiencies that the United States Government (already uneasily aware of the possible implications of Resolution 1514[XV]) was stimulated into unwonted activity. The Kennedy Administration, recently installed in Washington, was responsive to invitations to promote development in America's Pacific and Caribbean dependencies. No dependency was needier than Micronesia. Locally raised revenues were almost negligible, the economy stagnant since the eviction of the Japanese. The inept architectural reconstruction had earned the Trust Territory the nickname of the Rust Territory; bridges and roads had crumbled or disappeared into the landscape. Interisland communications were poor. Though the costs of administration had greatly increased since 1951, Congressional appropriations had never exceeded seven million dollars a year for the territory (apart from the Saipan District under the Navy). The Territory was still governed from Guam, and had no central legislature except the High Commissioner.

The return of the Marianas to civilian rule was accompanied by an increase in the budget ceiling for the territory to fifteen million dollars, though the first installment of the new subsidy was not received till May 1963. The new High Commissioner, appointed in 1961, made thirty-eight trips to Washington in four years, mostly in order to raise funds. Micronesia throve on adverse publicity. Fortunately the criticism from the Trusteeship Council has never yet been so harsh as to be counterproductive. And the irate, pained, or half-humorous American critic [14] has been, on the whole, a useful ally to the administrative friends of Micronesia. Among these friends are, of course, the small staff of the Office of Territories in the Department of the Interior. This Office has administrative responsibility for the affairs of the Virgin Islands, American Samoa, Guam, Micronesia, and a constellation of tiny islets (mostly without permanent inhabitants) under American authority in the Pacific. It maintains direct relations with the chief executives in the territories for which it is responsible, and a primary task of its Director is to exercise tactful influence over the competent Congressional bodies, notably the House of Representatives Subcommittee on Territorial and Insular Affairs. The limits of its influence are, however, circumscribed. It is perhaps enough to say that for fiscal year 1968 the House Committee on Appropriations recommended $1.412 billion for the Interior Department; more than half of this sum was to go to the Office of Oil and Gas, and just $45 million to the Office of Territories, or about 40% of the cost of a building which housed a Saturn V space rocket. There are also enlightened officials in the State Department, concerned with the affairs and future of the Trust Territory. The Department of Defense and the National Security Council will undoubtedly play an important part in any decision regarding its ultimate status.

One must add that although constituent legislation for the Territory is still by means of Secretarial Orders made by the Secretary of the Interior, it would be imprudent, to say the least, for the Executive to make any such Order without the concurrence of the appropriate Congressional bodies in Washington. Time after time the United Kingdom Parliament has accepted, sometimes grudgingly, a *fait accompli* presented to it after negotiations or a constitutional conference held between the Commonwealth or Colonial Office and the Government of a British dependent territory. Life is less simple within the American constitutional system, particularly in view of the independent initiative of the legislative branch in financial matters.

III

The year 1964 is the most useful point for taking stock of progress in Micronesia. This was the year of the second United Nations Visiting Mission (composed of members from New Zealand, Nationalist China, Liberia and the United Kingdom) to address itself exclusively to that territory. By this time the Territory was administratively organized in its present six districts, the Marianas, Yap, Palau, Truk, Ponape and the Marshalls, with territorial headquarters in Saipan. The population was about 85,000. The idea that the territory ought to be left as an anthropological museum or a picturesque backwater had been discarded. The need for action to promote political, social and economic development had been accepted in Washington, but only the first fruits of the new approach were apparent.

The report of the Visiting Mission [15] consisted of a general introduction, noting both the exceptional difficulties standing in the way of development and the dismal consequences of the years of neglect. Chapters were included on educational and social advancement, war damage and land claims, economic advancement, political advancement and the future of the territory.

The biggest advance was taking place in the field of education. Hitherto there had been one good public secondary school, the Pacific Islands Central School in Ponape, serving the whole territory; several good mission schools; and a number of elementary and intermediate public schools varying from the mediocre to the execrable. "The blind were leading the blind." [16] The poor qualifications of local teachers, the defective equipment of school buildings, and inadequate standards of English, imposed almost insuperable handicaps on all but the most gifted and ambitious students. But things were looking up. Following a decision to adopt a crash program, expenditure on education had dramatically risen to ten million dollars for fiscal year 1964, mainly on new classrooms and teachers' housing. There was to be free education, conducted entirely in the English language from elementary to high school. Each district was to have its own high school. Teachers' training was to be accelerated, with a large number of teachers imported from the United States. But vocational and technical training languished, as it does still. Despite the important advances since 1962, one has the impression that a widely diffused liberal arts type of education, related to a fundamentally alien culture and remote from the realities of everyday life in Micronesia, may create new problems for Micronesia until the emphasis is shifted towards the needs of the environmental setting.

Health services were patchy and inadequate by western standards. The fact was that groups of small isolated communities presented intractable problems, and if standards of public health were wholly unsatisfactory, the indigenous population, which had increased only slightly under the Japanese mandate, would not have increased by 40,000 in twenty years of American occupation and rule. In 1966 a WHO mission was to offer harsher criticism, especially on the prevalence of tuberculosis and the poverty of general sanitation.[17] American administrators are receptive to this kind of challenge.

The Mission found it hard to say kind things about the state of the economy. Years of governmental neglect, the exclusion or discouragement of outside investment and settlement, the sluggish tempo of life, the dearth of local resources, skills and enterprise, failure to encourage effective use of available resources and the absence of a territorial development plan, had conduced to a depressing atmosphere of stagnation. The new priority given to liberal education might even aggravate these problems without fresh approaches to economic problems, creating more local employment. Copra remained overwhelmingly the main source of export revenue, but the priority given to the expansion of local food production was far too low. Micronesia was "one of the great fishing grounds of the world," [18] but its resources had remained virtually untapped under American rule.

The production of handicrafts was encouraged subject, however, to import duties in the United States. Roads and housing were in a sorry state. Interisland shipping services, power plants and water supply were insufficient to meet modest demands. Micronesia required a large-scale economic plan with extensive local involvement in its formulation and execution. But the Mission thought a major drive to attract tourists premature, a distraction from more urgent issues, and perhaps a source of social disruption.[19]

The United States Government did not drag its feet. It commissioned a leading firm of economic consultants to prepare a long-term plan for the Territory. It announced arrangements for a big influx of Peace Corps personnel into the Territory to assist in education and development. And it sought a grant of $172 million from Congress for a five-year program of development.

The last request was turned down, though annual appropriations by Congress were increased. The Peace Corps arrangements proceeded. The Nathan Report on an economic development plan for Micronesia was published in December 1966. The report,[20] a splendid source of factual information, provided some acute analyses of the problems. Unfortunately its authors were overly impressed by the philosophy of Adam Smith [21] and convinced of the paramount virtue of self-help. If perpetual economic dependency on the United States—a not unattractive prospect for many Micronesians [22]—were to be averted, it was essential to develop the private rather than the dominant public sector. This involved concentration on agriculture, fisheries, and tourism and its infrastructure—a list of priorities with which many of the Report's critics would agree. But in the eyes of its authors, to achieve this desideratum it would be necessary to attract foreign investors, introduce foreign managers, technicians and skilled labor, make land more freely alienable to private developers, concentrate on the population centers, and offer disincentives to the backward-looking 30% who obstinately preferred to dwell on remote outer islands.

The Nathan Report was an interesting economic exercise, innocent of social psychology and charged with political dynamite. The Administration has come to recognize that what was good for General Motors, or Hawaii, or Micronesia under Japanese rule, would not be acceptable to the Micronesians in the 1960s. But the report did help to persuade the Administration that the road to salvation might lie through tourism, and that the district centers should be the main development areas.

The 1964 Visiting Mission's comments on political advancement began on an optimistic note. "Micronesia . . . is now welding itself into a unified people . . . a national consciousness has begun to evolve." [23] But it had to conclude "that the conditions for self-determination do not yet exist." [24] Both the Administration and the populace had extremely vague ideas about ultimate status. The Mission drew attention to the possibility of free association as an alternative to independence or integration with the United States, brushing aside Saipanese separatist demands, and indeed recommending transfer of territorial headquarters from Saipan to Truk. It made a number of useful comments on the composition and functions of the proposed territorial legislature, the Congress of Micronesia. It questioned the appropriateness of the separation of powers doctrine in a Micronesian context. As well as calling for a more rapid Micronization of the higher levels of the civil service, it looked forward to the day when there would be a Micronesian Chief Executive. We shall consider constitutional and political developments from 1965 onwards in the next chapter.

NOTES

1. 8 U.N. Treaty Series 190.

2. 61 Stat. 397.

3. 68 Stat. 330.

4. The presently effective instrument of delegation is Executive Order No. 11021, made on May 8, 1962 (27 Federal Register 4409).

5. An amendment to the proposed draft agreement, deleting the words "as an integral part of the United States," was moved by the Soviet Union and accepted by the United States on the understanding that the deletion of the words would not diminish its authority in the territory. However, the long-term psychological effect of this amendment may not have been insignificant.

6. Cf. Richard Barrett Lowe, *Problems in Paradise* (Pageant Press, 1968), xvii, pointing out that the first four civilian governors of American Samoa (after the termination of naval rule) had resigned between June 1952 and May 1953.

7. E. J. Kahn, Jr., *A Reporter in Micronesia* (New York: W. W. Norton, 1965), 39–40.

8. Kahn, *op. cit.,* 76.

9. For recent articles on Bikini, see Hill Williams, "Bikini Nine Years Later," *Science Journal* (London), No. 4 (April 1967), 45–53; Nicholas Wollaston, "Return to Bikini," *Sunday Times Magazine* (London), Octo-

ber 27, 1968, pp. 56–66. Resettlement began in 1969.

10. Kahn, *op. cit.,* 80–82.

11. See Report of the United Nations Visiting Mission, 1967(T/1658), para. 222.

12. Constitutional and administrative developments in this period are briefly surveyed in the Report of the United Nations Visiting Missions to the Trust Territory of the Pacific Islands for 1961(T/1582) and 1964-(T/1628), and by Whitney D. Perkins, *Denial of Empire,* 323–329. See also generally Robert Trumbull, *Paradise in Trust* (New York: William Sloane, 1959).

13. Report, T/1582 (Trusteeship Council, Official Records, Twenty-Seventh Session, Supp. No. 2).

14. Theodore F. Henning, *Buritis in Paradise* (Greenwich Book Publishers, 1961) belongs to the first category; Willard Price, *America's Paradise Lost* (John Day Co., 1966), Eugene J. McCarthy, *The Limits of Power* (New York: Holt, Rinehart & Winston, 1967), VIII, and Senator Mike Mansfield, the majority leader in the Senate (*Congressional Record,* July 18, 1967, S9794–9796) belong to the second category; E. J. Kahn, *A Reporter in Micronesia* (New York: W. W. Norton, 1965) belongs to the third.

15. T/1628 (Trusteeship Council: Official Records: Thirty-First Session, Supp. No. 2).

16. Report, §22.

17. Report, U.N. Document T/1647 (1966).

18. Report, §145.

19. Report §§158–160.

20. *Economic Development Plan for Micronesia* (Washington, D.C.: Robert R. Nathan Associates Inc., 1966).

21. See especially Vol. 1, p. 55.

22. Report, Vol. 1, p. 85.

23. *Ibid.,* §194.

24. *Ibid.,* §298.

CHAPTER 10

Micronesia: The Congress and the Administration

In the multitude of counsellors there is safety.
(Proverbs, xi, 14)

Money is indeed the most important thing in the world. . . .
(George Bernard Shaw)

I

The United Nations Visiting Mission of 1964 envisaged the new Congress of Micronesia as an instrument for unification of the territory.[1] How far have these hopes been fulfilled? This is a question that will recur in the following chapters.

The Congress of Micronesia was constituted in pursuance of Secretarial Order No. 2882, made in 1964 after extensive discussions in Micronesia and Washington. It replaced the advisory Council of Micronesia, which had consisted of two delegates from each of the six administrative districts. The Congress is bicameral: the Senate has two members from each district, holding their seats for four years, half retiring every second year; the House of Representatives (formerly the House of Delegates) has twenty-one members, elected biennially. Elections are held in November. In 1969 the Congress decided to remain a bicameral body. A single chamber could hardly fail to work more efficiently. But the existing structure provides the less populous districts (Yap, the Marianas and Palau) with more than proportionate representation. A reform giving offense to all three could hardly have been undertaken. In the House of Representatives representation is roughly in accordance with population, but the Marianas are slightly over-represented and Truk, the most populous district, is slightly under-represented.[2] Yap has two members, the Marianas and Palau three each, the Marshalls and Ponape four each and Truk five. The two Houses sit in adjacent, modest chambers in a small single-story building complex on Capitol Hill, within a mile of the High Commissioner's Headquarters.

To be eligible for election to Congress a person must be a citizen of the Trust Territory for at least five years, and not less than twenty-five years of age. He must also have been resident for at least a year in the district where he stands as a candidate. The franchise is exercizable by all citizens of the Trust Territory over the age of eighteen years. For five years after the establishment of the Congress, territorial or district government employees were eligible for election. This provision (reminiscent of the rule formerly in force for indigenous Fijians) had been included in the Secretarial Order because of the dearth of suitably qualified candidates; in 1968 nine out of twelve Senators were employed by the Administration.

Regular sessions of Congress were to last for not more than thirty days. Compensation of members was fixed at sixteen dollars a day, plus traveling allowances. These rules were in force till the end of 1968.[3]

The proceedings of the Congress must be conducted in English, but a member not fluent may use an interpreter. In practice all members now speak English fluently. In 1968 only one, the venerable Chief Petrus Mailo of Truk, used an interpreter, and he was himself able to follow most of the proceedings conducted in English; he did not stand for reelection later that year. The transaction of proceedings in English has had an important effect on the composition of Congress; nearly all candidates have been youngish, educated men. In 1968 only one Senator was over forty-five, seven were between thirty-five and forty-five, and four were under thirty-five; the average age was about thirty-seven; all had had some form of further education outside the Territory, mostly in Hawaii. The average age of the House of Representatives was two years older, but this was explained by the presence of Chief Petrus among the members. In fact only two were over forty-five, seven were between thirty-five and forty-five, twelve were under thirty-five. It appeared that twelve of the twenty-one had had further education outside the Territory. It was generally recognized that membership of the House carried with it slightly less prestige than membership of the Senate. Several Congressmen were graduates of the Pacific Islands Central School. Since a majority of members were in the thirty-five to forty-five age group and many of them had shared educational experiences in Ponape or Hawaii (especially at the University or the East-West Center), they had more in common with one another than one might have expected. In more than one sense they were able to speak the same language. Inevitably, they were influenced politically by their experience in the United States. From observing formal and informal proceedings, and from private discussions, one formed the very clear opinion that the quality of the members was good and the level of sophistication higher than in some other Pacific territories. This impression is supported by Professor Norman Meller of the University of Hawaii, a leading contemporary authority on political developments in the Pacific.[4]

II

The Congress is precluded from legislating inconsistently with United States international agreements, United States laws extending to the Territory, Executive Orders of the President and Orders of the Secretary of the Interior, or the territorial bill of rights. It cannot, therefore, amend the constitution, which is embodied in Secretarial Orders. It can, however, recommend amendments to the High Commissioner by a two-thirds' majority vote in each House. Nor can the Congress tax United States or territorial government property, or impose fiscal burdens on the intraterritorial transportation of goods. With minor exceptions, its appropriations power extends only to locally raised revenues. The overwhelming bulk of the Territory's revenue is derived from the United States Government. In October 1968 the United States Congress raised the appropriations ceiling for fiscal years 1970 to 1971,[5] to the very substantial sum of fifty million dollars a year.[6] Everyone in Micronesia would be both delighted and surprised if such a sum were in fact to be appropriated for the Territory; appropriations have adopted a disconcerting habit of falling well short of the amounts previously authorized. The appropriations actually authorized for fiscal year 1970 proved to be forty-one million dollars.

The High Commissioner's [7] power to enact legislation designated by him as urgent and not passed by Congress was removed by the Fourth Amendment to Order No. 2882 in July 1968. But he retains power to recommend the enactment of legislation and a power of veto, including an item veto in respect of appropriation bills, and a "pocket veto." [8] If he returns a bill, his veto may be overridden by two-thirds' majorities in both Houses. If the returned bill is not then approved by the High Commissioner within twenty days, it goes to the Secretary of the Interior, whose decision is final. As under other American-style constitutions, the power of veto is no mere formality. In 1967 seven bills were vetoed, and in 1968 no fewer than 14 of the 51 bills passed by the Congress were disapproved (six of them by pocket veto). Among the bills directly vetoed in 1968 was one previously pocket vetoed in 1967. This was an Eminent Domain Bill, attaching restrictive conditions to the Administration's acquisition of land for public purposes. The context was one of resentment at past military expropriation of scarce resources. For good measure, the Congress passed an identical "new" bill in the same terms; this too was vetoed.[9]

This recital suggests that executive-legislative relations in Micronesia are not uniformly harmonious. Admittedly, Senate Joint Resolution No. 28 of 1968 expressed "pride and faith" in the High Commissioner; but not all is sweetness and light. One notes, for example, that the Administration is not very successful in securing the adoption of its legislative program. In 1967 only ten out of 25 administration bills were passed into law. Criticism of the Administration or its laws covered a wide front in 1968: the retention of land for military activities in the Marshalls; slow Micronization of the civil service; salary differentials between American and Micronesian employees in the civil service; the fact that employees of the United States Government were employed at all in the Trust Territory Government; those recruited outside the Territory should be employed only under contract; inadequacy of grants to Micronesian students in Guam, and inadequate post-graduate job opportunities; the unavailability of sufficient funds for a variety of development and rehabilitation projects; and so forth. Most of the bills disapproved by the High Commissioner in 1968 were designed to change the existing law relating to public and private lands, to increase aid for higher education, and to reform the civil service.

These indications of tension and conflict ought not, perhaps, be taken too seriously. They express frustration rather than embittered opposition and alienation. They are intermingled with expressions of gratitude and appreciation. House Joint Resolution No. 11 of 1968 requested the High Commissioner to investigate the feasibility of having a permanent representative in Washington to represent the interests of the people of Micronesia (as the interests of the Guamanians were already represented). But they do point to a gulf between the elected representatives and their Government which strikingly exemplifies a basic defect in Washington's export model. There is no effective link between the executive and the legislature. It is apparently unthinkable to have a Cabinet composed partly of officials and partly of legislators. All members of the Cabinet must be members of the Administration. It is also apparently unthinkable to dilute the top level of the Administration by introducing a less qualified or experienced Micronesian instead of or in addition to an American head of department. In 1969 no departmental head was a Micronesian. One Micronesian had been brought into the Cabinet as personal aide to the High Commissioner, and another was a District Administrator. But Micronesians still had no significant voice in the shaping of policy. That the major policy decisions were made not in Saipan but in Washington, D.C. could be conceded; that the Territorial Government was mindful of the voices of the Congress of Micronesia was manifest; yet it seemed highly incongruous to a British observer that so much talent in the legislature was obliged to express itself by remonstrance and supplication when some of it could have been more constructively employed in the shaping of territorial programs. The President of the Senate and the Speaker of the House of Representatives, and the two floor leaders, were not closely identified with the Administration. If deeply ingrained prejudices about the proper constitutional structure for America's wards rule out a ministerial system, it is still important to devise informal machinery for frequent consultations between departmental heads and an elected group of Congressmen on issues of general policy, consultations not restricted to when Congress is in session.

Five factors have hitherto averted serious confrontations between executive and legislature. First, senior members of the Administration have made themselves readily available for interrogation by congressional committees and are not, on the whole, socially remote.

Second, although a parliamentary executive is taboo, a high proportion of Congressmen have been government employees, and this must have tended to soften criticism; in 1968 a senior official found himself called to testify before a congressional committee including three of his subordinates. But the Fourth Amendment to the Secretarial Order, made in July 1968, now disqualifies employees of the territorial government and of district administrations from serving as members of Congress. The gulf may yawn wider. Third, Congressmen know only too well where the power of the purse lies. Economic dependence begets political dependence. But it can also engender other attitudes, leading to counteraccusations of ingratitude and fecklessness. We shall touch upon financial relationships in the next section. Fourth, there is no all-Micronesian political party, and no sign of one about to emerge. Local political parties have existed for several years in Saipan and Palau, the two most sophisticated districts. Elsewhere, all members are independents, running for election on the basis of local issues, personal standing, or both. The Administration is unlikely to become uncomfortable unless a large party, excluded from power, establishes itself in strength in Congress. Fifth—and this is a possibility that cannot be dismissed—a movement for Micronesian independence might develop along lines, not necessarily bounded by the discipline of a political party, which would seriously embarrass the Territorial Government.

III

As we have noted, the appropriations power of the Congress is limited almost entirely to revenues raised locally by the Territorial Government. Since well over 95% of the Territory's revenue is derived from grants made by the United States, this is not a significant sum of money. Indeed it is little more than one million dollars. The largest components are the export taxes on copra and scrap metal, import tax and motor vehicle fuel excise duty (but more than half of these taxes are refunded to the district legislatures), rentals and sundry reimbursements. Under the terms of Public Law 1–6, which divides the taxing power between the Territory, the districts and the municipalities, it is possible for Congress to levy a tax on incomes. But there is in fact no territorial income tax or corporation tax, and import duties are not high. The salaries of the some five-hundred

American officials serving in the Territory are taxed in the United States. Potential new sources of revenue are thus untapped and existing sources are insufficiently exploited. In 1968, after Congress had met its operating expenses, made grants to the districts and appropriated sums for recurrent purposes such as social security benefits, it was left with barely $300,000, a trivial sum. Projects and capital improvement requests submitted by various Congressmen would have cost more than five times this sum. Given the strength of district particularism and the fact that the policy-making executive branch of government is non-Micronesian, this state of affairs is hardly conducive to the prestige of Congress or to the building of a new nation. It was greatly to the credit of Congress then, that it allocated most of the residue to a new Micronesian scholarship fund. The bill passed for this purpose encroached upon the functions of the existing scholarships board and was, alas, vetoed.

If Congress is poor, the districts are poorer and the municipalities are poorer still. The creation of Congress and the enactment of Public Law 1–6 almost decimated the revenue of Saipan Municipality, hardly diminishing separatist sentiment. The financial resources of the municipalities barely enable them to discharge their responsibilities for the maintenance of law and order, and are manifestly inadequate, as a visitor will immediately find, for the upkeep of minor roads. But although lack of money inhibits the work of district and municipal legislative bodies and administrations, the introduction of representative and elective institutions by the United States has stimulated interest (often steeped in frustration) in public affairs throughout the Territory. And the unitary nature of the territorial constitution has at least focused interest on what happens when Congress meets in July.

Up to now, the Congress has had little influence over the Administration's budget. Estimates are submitted a year or more in advance by District Administrators and departmental heads, and eventually filter through to the High Commissioner. Before putting his final requests to the Secretary of the Interior for federal funds, the High Commissioner must prepare a preliminary budget plan and lay it before the Congress of Micronesia in joint session. Congress may make recommendations with respect to the expenditure of federally appropriated funds, which the High Commissioner must either adopt or transmit to the Interior Department. The budget for fiscal year 1969 gave the highest priorities to education (including new classrooms and, at last, vocational training), health and sanitation services (hospitals and water supplies), and an electric power plant. If development of tourism were to salvage the economy, then the infrastructure had to be strengthened. But major improvements of roads and harbors would have to be postponed for another two years. And the development of agriculture and fisheries had priority. Despite grumbling and criticism, Congress grew resigned to the fact that major policy decisions had already been made—most likely by Washington. In any event, there could be no real question of seeking a reduction of the executive budget. The United States Congress in 1968 had insisted on a reduction of six billion dollars in Federal Government expenditure in return for its consent to 10% income tax surcharge. The idea that the Congress of Micronesia might make even the gesture of a comparable recommendation is ludicrous. The goose may be chided, but it must not be made so disgruntled as to flutter away to lay its golden egg on a distant doorstep.

IV

To evaluate the Congress of Micronesia after only five years of operation is not altogether satisfactory. Most of its weaknesses have already been indicated. It is subordinate (though not subservient) to an irremovable non-Micronesian executive. Its members have little share in shaping policy, except insofar as they may have been government employees. It lacks adequate funds. It can do no more than exert marginal pressure on those determining the allocation of United States aid. There are no Micronesia-wide political parties. There is no clear sense of direction. The High Commissioner's power of veto is a reality. Even when it is overridden, the final decision rests in Washington. The power base of members of Congress lies in their respective districts. None of these districts constitutes a powerful pressure group, and interests are often discordant, particularly as funds are scarce. Its sessions are brief, and in August the members disperse to their own islands.

Is the Congress of Micronesia anything more than a talking-shop? The answer must be tentative, but a visitor might offer a cautiously affirmative response. In the first place, the level of debate is, on the whole, good, with many thoughtful contributions. Members tend to be well educated, aware of one another's difficulties, aware of the world around them despite inadequate news media.[10] Second, they appreciate that despite the islands' economic dependence, America needs Micronesia. America can be embarrassed at the United Nations if they adopt a common front and assert themselves in a well-calculated manner. Petitions can be addressed to the Trusteeship Council. Representations can be made to Visiting Missions, whose reports are taken quite seriously at the United Nations. The two Congressmen who accompany the American delegation to the Trusteeship Council as special advisers each year do not talk like obedient puppets. And there is always the Committee of Twenty-Four lurking in the background. These outlets would be available even if there were no Congress of Micronesia, but its existence maximizes the indirect pressure on the Administration to accelerate economic and political development. One of the most interesting and important moves in the history of Micronesia was the decision of the Congress in 1966 to set up its own Future Political Status Commission. Third, Congress has acquired a good deal of prestige in Micronesia. This was made clear in 1968 when principal chiefs from Yap and Palau arrived to observe proceedings, hold discussions with the Administration while Congress was in session, or testify before Congressional committees on bills in order to put pressure on the Administration for local legislative changes. It was made clearer when late in 1968 Amendment No. 4 to the Secretarial Order had disqualified government officers and employees and members of district legislatures from membership of Congress—an obeisance to the separation of powers doctrine—and had provided for a salary of $3,500 per annum for Congressmen.[11] At the same time the length of regular legislative sessions was increased from thirty to forty-five days, with provision for an additional regular session in January of up to fifteen days in alternate years. There were many who had then anticipated a mass exodus from Congress, for the salary was not handsome even by Micronesian standards, and few members had other income. But there was no mass exodus, and as far as is known only two of those who stood down did so in order to retain public office; one other senator resigned so as to remain a medical officer. Twenty-two out of the twenty-seven incumbents whose term had expired stood for reelection. Fourthly, Congress is a meeting point for leaders from the several districts. No doubt members are reminded of what divides them as well as what unites them; no doubt social contacts, say in the bar of the Royal Taga Hotel, are as important as political contacts. Micronesia cannot exist as more than a geographical expression in the absence of meaningful personal association. And the sessions of Congress institutionalize that association.

Despite its present inadequacies, only Congress can forge Micronesia into a nation. A few comments can be made on its method and procedure. As one might expect, it is modeled on the pattern of an American state legislature. The Administration arranged for instruction in the appropriate techniques as well as observing legislative proceedings in Hawaii. Visitors are apt to find themselves introduced and applauded from the floor. The atmosphere is informal, almost casual: Congressmen normally wear open-necked shirts; in 1968 ties were donned only for the High Commissioner's State of the Territory Message. Unlike the Governor's corresponding message in the Virgin Islands, it was devoid of patriotic American rhetoric and was not preceded by a military tune or the Star-Spangled Banner. The High Commissioner was duly applauded. The arrangement of legislative business was not particularly efficient, and by midsession one-hundred bills and seventy-three resolutions had been introduced in the House of Representatives alone. There was duplication of effort with the Senate, and it was clear that the existence of two Houses was justifiable only on the grounds of political expedience. The Congress was lucky to have a very able, if overworked, Legislative Counsel, Kaleb Udui, who performed prodigious feats of draftsmanship, aided by energetic Peace Corps volunteers. Most of the district legislatures also have members of the Peace Corps as draftsmen. Some degree of coordination was achieved in the week preceding the session, through informal discussions and committee hearings. A bill or resolution is normally referred to a standing committee—there are now five standing committees in the Senate and six in the House, provision being made by Standing Orders for fair representation of the several districts—and if a bill is reported favorably out of committee, it goes to its second and final reading. There is provision for joint conferences in the event of disagreement. Neither House can override the other. Amid the welter of confusion and improvisation, what is surprising is not that the achievements are modest but that so much constructive work is done.

NOTES

1. Report, T/1628, §250.

2. See Norman Meller, "Districting a New Legislature in Micronesia," 7, *Asian Survey* (1967), 457–468.

3. For the present position, see p. 155, *post*.

4. *New Guinea Research Bulletin* (No. 22, January 1968), VI.

5. The fiscal year begins on July 1 of the preceding calendar year.

6. 82 Stat. 1213. This Act also authorized an increase of $5 million for fiscal year 1969 to 40 million, and an annual sum not in excess of $10 million to be disbursed by the Secretary of the Interior in his discretion for relief made necessary by major disasters in the territory.

7. For his relationship with the Secretary of the Interior and the Office of Territories, see Part II of Secretarial Order No. 2918 of December 27, 1968.

8. The High Commissioner may return a bill with his objections within ten days after it has been presented to him for signature; if he does not return it within ten days, it becomes law, *unless* Congress adjourns in the meantime. Since the duration of sessions is limited by the Secretarial Orders, the High Commissioner may in effect veto a bill by keeping it in his "pocket" if the bill is presented to him less than ten days before the end of the session. But he is empowered to sign a bill after an adjournment, provided that he so acts within thirty days after the bill has been presented to him.

9. Prior to Secretarial Order No. 2918 of December 27, 1968, a veto could be overridden only in the next session, before the expiry of fourteen months. The 1968 order preserved the rights of Congress to reconsider in 1969 bills returned by the High Commissioner in 1968.

10. Radio bulletins are the main news source. There is no Micronesia-wide newspaper except a narrowly distributed official news sheet, though there is now a good illustrated quarterly review of territorial affairs. The few district journals carry little information. Imported American journals and newspapers are extremely scarce. In Saipan, journals from Guam are obtainable.

11. The Speaker of the House and the President of the Senate were to receive an extra $500 a year. Traveling and subsistence expenses were to be paid to members of Congress. See Secretarial Order No. 2918, §18; and p. 187, note 1, *post*.

CHAPTER 11

Micronesia: Unity in Diversity?

The mould is not yet made—perhaps
That can unite and make my people one.
(H. D. Carberry)

I

"He travels the fastest who travels alone," wrote Kipling. In Micronesia's jet-age, this is not necessarily true. But the words of Francis Bacon are as sound as they were in 1597: "He that travelleth into a country, before he hath some entrance into the language, goeth to school, and not to travel." And when one records his impressions of a cursory visit to a far-flung domain, what he has to say will inevitably appear superficial or derivative. Here I propose to make some discursive observations on the districts of Micronesia, including some further comments on the Marianas and Yap.

Micronesia has its own flag, its own citizenship, and its own national holiday, Micronesia Day, July 12, commemorating the inauguration of the Congress of Micronesia. This cluster of islands exists as a political entity because of outside forces—Japan, the League of Nations, the United States, the United Nations. Without superimposed pressure the Territory might well fragment into six, eight, or more separate parts.

The unity of Micronesia seems to be at least as fragile as the voluntary federation of the British West Indies. The elements of diversity, and the distances between islands, are far greater, and conflicts of interest no less, though in Micronesia the local political boss has yet to build an empire. Enforced confederation—and let no one doubt that it is enforced—may yet induce a degree of unity, predicated on a realistic appraisal of self-interest, which might, in turn, survive a transition to self-rule.

Only during the 1960s has any serious attempt been made to persuade the Micronesians of their political future as a nation. Conditioned to the idea of dependence by long years of subordination, remote from one another and from the currents of anticolonialist sentiment that had swirled through other continents, they have had to be led into the paths of righteousness. In political matters, prominent Micronesians have shed their apathy and lost their fear of the unknown. They want to govern themselves and they are beginning to force the pace. Beyond this, they are uncertain of their ultimate status. They are aware of their paternalistic benefactor's desire for them to cling together and remain under America's protection; aware too, of America's apprehension lest matters get out of control. They acknowledge Micronesia's weakness in resources and technical skills, its uncertainty as to ends and means, its dedication to autonomy rather than unity. In this fluid situation, an initiative pointing unequivocally to a specific destination may indeed resolve doubts; yet there remains a danger that it may upset the delicate balance and precipitate internecine conflict and disarray.

II

The economy of the Marshalls rests on coconut production supplemented by American military expenditure on Kwajalein and Eniwetok, which has attracted a relatively well paid indigenous labor force. Among the Marshallese there are extremes of discontent with American rule—deep resentment at the use of the territory as a nuclear testing ground, with consequential forced evacuations of small islands and exposure to radioactive fall-out, and at the conduct of other military experiments in a district covering barely seventy square miles of land—coupled with a keen appreciation of the material benefits of American presence. The more astute Marshallese realize their potentially valuable bargaining counter in their relations with the United States. Their most influential political leader, Amata Kabua, formerly floor leader and now President of the Senate, is nothing if not astute. Although the Marshalls are far-flung atolls, they are less remote and more aware of the world around them than are some of the other districts of the Territory. Traders, whalers and missionaries bestowed their offerings upon the Marshallese before the Germans, the Japanese and the Americans came to reorder their lives. Majuro, the district center, is as close to Hawaii as to Saipan; Nauru lies but a few hundred miles away. If one is looking for the end of the earth, one will not find it in the Marshalls.

Some residents in Micronesia regard Ponape as the most remote of all the districts. Perhaps this is because communications have been relatively poor—till 1969 the district was still accessible only by boat or seaplane—and perhaps it is because Ponape is less homogeneous than any other district. Apart from the anomaly of a southern Polynesian fringe, there are tensions and linguistic differences between the two main islands, Ponape and Kusaie. The people of Kusaie feel neglected by the Ponape District Administration and Legislature, and want to be constituted as a separate district, an aim endorsed by a joint resolution of the Congress of Micronesia in 1968. Both Ponape and Kusaie are high, wet and luxuriant islands. Their agricultural potential has not been adequately developed. Coconuts, yams, taro, breadfruit and bananas are more than sufficient for subsistence. There are modest experiments in the cultivation of pepper on Ponape, with good prospects for rice and cacao, as well as substantial resources of valuable timber. But agricultural development maintains low priority. In June 1968 the new Trust Territory Farm Institute on Ponape was actually closed for lack of funds. Tourists will certainly make their way to Ponape, attracted by its natural beauty and the massive ancient stone ruins of Nan Madol. They may, however, "find, not a cultivated garden island, but a green, fallow hulk." [1]

Ponape, though seriously underdeveloped, with particularly atrocious roads (now gradually improved by self-help),[2] is not conspicuously "backward." From the district come some of Micronesia's most prominent younger citizens: Leo Falcam, first Micronesian to sit in the Cabinet; Bailey Olter, energetic and imaginative senator; Bethwel Henry, Speaker of the House of Representatives and Hirosi Ismael, an intelligent and sophisticated young doctor, till recently a senator.[3] One has the impression that the Ponapeans, more than most, appreciate the advantages of a united Micronesia and the dangers of insular separatism.

The Trukkese knew better days under the Japanese, when the Imperial Fleet lay at anchor in the massive Truk lagoon and a large commercial fishing industry throve. A district of small atolls, intensely cultivated but now over-populated, Truk has been less receptive to American influence than most parts of Micronesia. Educational attainments have been moderate although Truk used to be the site of the Pacific Islands Central School and still has a long-established and well-regarded mission boarding school serving the whole Territory. Few Trukkese have attained prominence in territorial affairs. Truk tends to be conservative, traditionalist and inward-looking (despite migration to the Marianas) and conforms more closely than some of its neighbors to the stereotypical South Sea Island cluster. It could exist independently only by auctioning its disused naval facilities.

The Palauans had also enjoyed a wider range of economic opportunities under the Japanese. Apt pupils, they acquired new technical skills to augment their traditional prowess in construction and pictorial art, developing a zeal for modernization. With the departure of the South Seas Administration from Koro, the exhaustion of mineral deposits and the incursion of the coconut Rhinoceros beetle, the economy shrivelled. But the Palauans swiftly accommodated themselves to the new order, making ample use of freedom of speech, seeking advancement in education—they have the best record of any district in higher education. There are Palauan migrant communities in all the other districts, closely knit,[4] industrious and thrustful, supplying specialized skills, goods and services; even the barmaids in Saipan and Yap seem to be mainly Palauans. The Palauans are sometimes spoken of as the Jews, the Gujeratis or the Ibos of the Pacific. And like those other energetic and cohesive minorities they tend to be unpopular with their less resourceful neighbors. That the Palauans are unusually attractive aggravates their offense. They deserve encouragement in their own islands. Clearly there is room for the further development of fisheries and constructional enterprises, and for agricultural progress on the large island of Babelthuap, despite the ever-present menace of the typhoon.[5] If Micronesia continues to exist as a political entity, it is from Palau that a high proportion of its leading citizens are likely to be drawn, assuming they overcome the initial disadvantage of being Palauan. Lazarus Salii, chairman of the Future Political Status Commission, formerly floor leader in the House and now a senator, and Kaleb Udui, Legislative Counsel to the Congress of Micronesia, are perhaps the best-known Micronesian figures on Capitol Hill. A number of other Palauans are making their mark in public life. And as the labor force is recruited for building the infrastructure of a tourist industry, Palauans will be there in strength.

III

The Mariana Islands District has a land area of some 183 square miles, slightly more than the Palau and Ponape Districts, and more than the combined land areas of the Marshall Islands, Truk and Yap districts. The islands are mainly high and volcanic, stretching northwards from Guam—Rota, Tinian, Saipan (the district center as well as territorial headquarters), and then a string of small islands, of which only Pagan, where there are coconut plantations, has any significant population. Saipan covers 47 square miles and has 9,000 inhabitants, about 80% of the population of the district; it lies within 100 miles of Guam. Descending to the airfield on Saipan, one sees the outlines of a disused airstrip on Tinian from which, late in July 1945, a B29 took off on a mission bound for Hiroshima.

Perhaps 70% of the people of the district are Chamorros. The remainder are mostly Carolinians, many of whom are descended from small immigrant communities who arrived in the Spanish and German periods during the late nineteenth and early twentieth centuries; there is also a number of Government employees from other districts working at territorial headquarters. The Japanese had no doubt that the Chamorros were a breed superior to the Kanakas. And the Nathan Report described them as being "by far the most sophisticated of all the Micronesians" [6]—a judgment questioned by many Palauans.

Saipan is a reasonably attractive, verdant, hilly island with magnificent sea views. Unlike any other of the larger islands in the Territory, it has good paved main roads, a by-product of the naval regime, though secondary roads are poor or nonexistent; if one turns right instead of left when emerging from the airfield, the roadway soon disappears into the jungloid growth that disfigures so much of the landscape. It has other facilities which are in short supply: cinemas; a supermarket; and a few well-appointed shops; as well as the first of the new sanitized, air-conditioned, American-style hotels (complete with an open-air swimming pool) which are to be erected in the six district centers. Even so, after taking into account the benefits of government employment and the spending power of high-salaried American officials and their families, Saipan has yet to recover from the devastation of Garapan in 1944 and the collapse of the agricultural economy with the departure of the Japanese. The debris of war still litters Saipan and its coastline. There are pillboxes and dugouts, a derelict sugar dock, a rusted American tank in the lagoon, a collection of crashed aircraft, captured guns and unexploded ammunition beyond the village of San Roque. A little farther stands the cliff from which hundreds of Japanese civilians leaped to mass suicide in order to avoid the shame of surrender; nearly thirty thousand Japanese troops commemorated by a small shrine outside the gates of the principal Catholic church are believed to have died in the battle.

Sophistication is, of course, a matter of degree. Apparent among the individualistic Chamorro professional men, politicians, traders and businessmen in the main township of Chalan Kanoa, it is less so in the small villages. In San Vicente, on Micronesia Day, a high school boy stood serving in a tiny store. Two elderly men were drinking beer. One, who spoke some English and had been to Honolulu, had been mightily impressed by Waikiki. The conversation was disrupted intermittently by chickens and a naked child, and by the raucous interjections of a woman speaking Chamorro. Outside lay the pathetic wooden ruins of collapsed shacks, smitten by Typhoon Jean three months earlier. A water buffalo cart lumbered along the road nearby.

The typhoon had struck suddenly on April 11. Gusts reached two-hundred miles an hour. Of the buildings on Saipan, 90% had been destroyed or damaged. Tinian, now the site of a cattle ranch, also suffered severely, and there was minor damage in Truk. The total cost of the damage was estimated at sixteen million dollars. The President of the United States declared the Northern Marianas a disaster area. The United States Congress authorized supplementary emergency appropriations. The Office of Emergency Planning supplied building materials. Priority was given to the reconstruction of public utilities, warehouses and schools, but five-hundred new houses, partly prefabricated, were erected in six months. Big brother was more than an advantage; he was a necessity.

Separatist sentiment in the Marianas has concerned Visiting Missions of the Trusteeship Council. In 1959 the Popular party was formed. Seeking union with Guam, it has been dominant in the district legislature and still more dominant in Saipan.[7] The main stronghold is in the Chamorro-speaking areas of Chalan Kanoa. Unofficial plebiscites, organized by the Popular party, show the majority in favor of its goal. Desire for union with Guam is based partly on ethnic, linguistic, cultural, and religious affinity; partly too, on the hope of sharing the economic benefits (in particular the high minimum wage rates) accruing to Guam as an incorporated territory and defense bastion of the United States. It is based on dissatisfaction with the relative anonymity of the Marianas in the new constitutional order. Furthermore, the Marianas' contribution to the Territory's revenue exceeds the funds granted them by the Congress of Micronesia.[8] And finally, there is resentment at the material diminution of the status and resources of the Saipan municipality.

This is a long and formidable list of reasons explaining the Marianas' lukewarm attitude towards the Trust Territory. Other factors, unquantifiable, have tended to offset the movement for union with Guam. It is well known that the Trusteeship Council and the Territorial Government are opposed to the movement. Guamanians are not universally popular. Union with Guam might leave Saipan a rather poor relation instead of a center of Government.

Some influential Saipanese find cultivation of special commercial links with Japan advantageous. A delegation from Saipan visited Japan seeking rehabilitation aid after the 1968 typhoon. There was some token financial assistance; and a group of young Japanese volunteers came to help in the restoration. It is interesting to note the number of Japanese cars and consumer goods in Saipan. There are Japanese receptionists and Japanese tourists at the Royal Taga Hotel. The main source of tourists must be Japan, which is less than two thousand miles away.[9]

Then there is the Territorial party, founded (first under the name of the Progressive party) to oppose the pro-Guamanian Popular party. It appears to draw its strength mainly from the middle class, government employees, and Carolinian immigrants, and from Rota, a separate administrative district while Saipan was under naval rule, but now feeling itself neglected by Saipan.

Tinian appears fairly evenly divided between the two parties. The leader of the Territorial party, Senator Olympia Borja, is emphatically pro-American; in 1968 he introduced (unsuccessfully) a resolution into the Senate requesting that Micronesians be permitted to join the United States armed forces. The party used to favor the Marianas' becoming a separate territory of the United States—in this sense it was as separatist as its rival—but now supports a united Micronesia closely linked with the United States. The party's position is fluid and options are open. But everyone thought it a minority party. True, it held one of the three seats for the Marianas in the Micronesian House of Representatives in 1968. Even this was attributed partly to personal factors and partly to some mild administrative gerrymandering.[10] It had one of the two Senate seats elected at large in the district as well, but this could be explained by divisions in the opponents' ranks.

In the summer of 1968 no one to whom the writer spoke thought that the Popular party commanded less than 60% of the vote in the Marianas. Some put its support substantially higher. Great, therefore, was the surprise when, at the general elections held late in 1968, the Territorial party won all four seats contested in the Marianas. Although the two new seats were won by very small majorities, the plain fact is that its candidates gathered 54% of the votes cast in the district. Whatever the best explanation of this remarkable result, and even if the set-back of the Popular party is only temporary, one can no longer regard the Marianas as a hopelessly intractable problem in the Micronesian context.

IV

The Yap district has the same land area as Truk but only a quarter of its population. The main land mass consists of four adjacent islands, usually called the Yap Islands proper. Somewhat confusingly, the largest of these islands, home of the district headquarters at Colonia, is itself called Yap. This group of islands (which would all be interconnected were there adequate bridges and causeways) lies about five-hundred-fifty miles southwest of Saipan and two-hundred-fifty miles northeast of Koror in Palau. The population is rather more than 4,000. Another 2,500 or more inhabitants of the district live in distant atolls, of which the best known are Ulithi and Woleai.

All travelers to Micronesia have paid special attention to the Yap islands. Doubtless one reason is that Yap is the only territory under American rule where the women go about bare-breasted and in fiber skirts; their photographs adorn illustrated brochures, books and articles.[11] But by 1968 the cotton dress, the blouse, and the brassiere had arrived, and of the few uncovered bosoms visible on Yap Island itself, most belonged to ladies from the outer islands. The men normally wear only loincloths.

Yap has attracted attention for a number of other reasons: its exceptional conservatism, its social structure and customs, its depopulation. The problem of depopulation is an interesting puzzle. We know that the indigenous population declined in Yap by 30% under Japanese rule between 1920 and 1937 while other districts were showing a modest increase.[12] We know too that it must have been considerably higher before the first contacts with Europeans in the nineteenth century, and that the decline continued in the early years of American rule, but has now been arrested. Low resistance to new diseases, and poor sanitation entailing high infant mortality, are part of the reason for the long decline. Mass melancholia and unnatural sexual practices are among the less plausible explanations. Perhaps the most persuasive suggestion is that of an American anthropologist, indicating that many young women practiced self-induced abortion furtively in the menstrual houses because bearing children would have abruptly terminated a free and easy life of license.[13] Today deserted villages and stone platforms, and the abundant crops, often rotting on the trees, testify to a more populous past and to a high agricultural potential.

Till the late nineteenth century the Yap Islands proper were the center of a small empire, levying tribute from the outer islands [14] and waging war from time to time on the Palauans. Within the islands, tribute was levied from those of low caste by those of higher caste. Indeed, a caste system, involving residential segregation, still persists in a modified form. So does an elaborate style of feudalism. Succession is patrilineal, and the authority of the household head is one to which deference must be paid. (Short stories recently written by high school pupils at Colonia portray the awful fates visited upon the daughter who stole the meat being prepared for her father's guest, and the boy who cut his grandfather's canoe adrift as a prank.) The men of the village have a communal assembly house, often handsomely constructed and decorated. The outer islands are administered by local chiefs, and individual chiefs exercise considerable influence in the Yap Islands proper.

Not only Americans but also many Micronesians regard Yap as

a picturesque anachronism. Picturesque it is indeed, not least because of its ceremonial feasts and dances; its tiny villages dispersed about the shore; and the celebrated *rai,* or stone money, hewn from Babelthuap in Palau and shipped back to Yap by O'Keefe in bulk; the massive limestone rings, symbolizing wealth and status, stand beside houses, public buildings and graves for display rather than for exchange. Whether it is thought anachronistic depends on individual values. Certainly Yap is conservative, traditionalist, and socially self-sufficient. Of all the districts it has remained by far the least receptive to Japanese and American innovations. In the modern Micronesian context it remains backward in education, in facility in the use of English, and in technical skills, generally underdeveloped and inward-looking. In political and constitutional development it has moved cautiously. Till 1968 only the Yap Islands proper and their municipalities had elected legislative bodies. The Congress of Micronesia then provided for the constitution of a district legislature. The inauguration of Congress in 1965 introduced elections to the district as a whole. One's impression is that having to work and compete with other districts induces apprehension among many Yapese, partly because they prefer keeping to themselves; partly because they doubt their own ability to compete successfully with, for example, the Saipanese and the Palauans. And the existence of universal franchise means that men of low caste, even Ulithian separatists, can be elected and voice dissatisfaction before strangers.

The Territorial Government's proposal that a major tourist hotel be constructed in each district center has made Yapese especially uneasy. In 1968 the Yap Islands legislature resolved that no such hotel be built for five years, and then only if 50% of the capital were locally subscribed. Since the cost of such a hotel was likely to be some six hundred thousand dollars, and no one knew the financial status of the Yapese—there is no bank in the district, except the so-called bank of stone-money at Balebat near Colonia—this was a case of hastening slowly. Most Yapese would prefer to avoid tourists encroaching on their privacy—a sentiment which the writer, as a tourist, can readily appreciate. Many of them, on the other hand, look forward to the creation of an infrastructure of tourism—roads, bridges, power supplies, pure running water, sewage disposal plant, and so forth—but do not relish the prospect of other Micronesian workers invading

Yap and then perhaps providing services once tourism is established. They shrink from loss of dignity. There is some awareness of what happened to the indigenous Hawaiians. At the same time the younger generation, especially, recognizes the poverty and backwardness of the island. They cannot afford to opt out altogether. An ideal solution would be to follow the example of Nauru. Unfortunately there are no phosphate deposits, and if there were, their masters and neighbors would not allow Yap to go it alone.

Colonia, the district center, no more than a village, is the headquarters of nearly all the coordinated public activities within the district. It has no paved roads; indeed, the only paved stretch in the district appears to be the airstrip, and the airfield is still surrounded by the wreckage of Japanese Zero fighters. Communications within the islands, though not intolerably bad—the Yapese have shown initiative in constructing tracks from local materials—are generally so poor as to impede the marketing of copra. (The writer can testify that a tour of the main island in a U-drive Datsun is a hazardous enterprise.) Everything is on a very small scale, except possibly O'Keefe's bar. Colonia straggles beside a polluted lagoon, separated by a rickety causeway from a shallow and narrow harbor, the inevitable war debris still rusting away. The shorelines are disfigured by the hovels of immigrant workers from other islands and laborers from villages outside the center, though the general standard of housing in Yap is satisfactory. In Colonia one rises and retires early. (In the villages where there is no power supply there are few inducements to stay up late, and no facilities for a student.) The tempo is slow and efficiency seldom high. In the district court,[15] presided over by a venerable and esteemed Yapese judge, the first case one morning had to be adjourned because after thirty-five minutes neither the prosecutor nor the defendant had appeared; a second criminal case was dismissed because the two complainants had signed one another's statements in error. And so the day moves along in Colonia, a day punctuated with the sound of sirens—summoning the employees of the public works department to their jobs, signaling the lunch hour and the end of the day's work, marking the curfew for minors, each blast followed by the half-hearted howling of dogs. Away in the villages the inhabitants cultivate their taro patches, go fishing, gather breadfruit, yams, coconuts and bananas, cook, eat, drink, chew betel nuts and spit the scarlet juice, smoke cigarettes, talk, make love, and go to bed.

There are glimpses of modernization: not only the airfield, the new school buses, the incursion of Peace Corps volunteers, the cinema specializing in horror films, and the young man sitting on the far side of the lagoon, strumming a Hawaiian guitar as he listended on his transistor radio, with a scarlet Honda motorcycle parked by his side, to a program presented by an American disc jockey. There is above all the sudden growth of the high school population, students of unfamiliar ideas in a liberal arts curriculum, students with few books at school and often none at home. Soon Yap will experience a phase of rising expectations. How can it fulfill them, or fulfill them without losing its ancient identity?

NOTES

1. P. F. Kluge, *Micronesian Reporter* (Fourth Quarter, 1968), 40. The *Micronesian Reporter,* now a basic source of reference for contemporary views and developments, is published by the Department of Public Affairs of the Trust Territory.

2. *Ibid.,* 17–20.

3. P. F. Kluge, *Micronesian Reporter* (Fourth Quarter, 1968). See pp. 3–11 for an unusually interesting interview with Dr. Ismael.

4. Cf. H. G. Barnett, *Being a Palauan* (New York: Holt, Rinehart & Winston, 1960).

5. In March 1967 about $5 million worth of damage was caused by Typhoon Sally. The Palauans have complained that less was done for them by the Administration than for the Saipanese after the typhoon of April 1968, and that they ought not to have been required to reimburse the Administration for the cost of materials supplied for the reconstruction of houses.

6. Report, Vol. 2, p. 385.

7. In 1968 it held all the seats on the Saipan municipal council, and eight of the eleven elected posts of district commissioner. The head of the municipality is an elected mayor. For a historical survey of municipal administration in the Marianas, see Robert R. Solenberger, "Continuity of Local Political Institutions in the Marianas," 23, *Human Organization* (1964), 53–60.

8. When a territorial income tax is imposed, this may aggravate the situation. On Saipanese separatism, see generally Reports of the United Nations Visiting Missions for 1961 (T/1582, §§55–69), 1964 (T/1628, §§245–248, 284–291) and 1967 (T/1658, §§321–324).

9. The territorial copra exports go almost entirely to Japan. The Territory has no other significant export market.

10. Cf. Norman Meller, "Districting a New Legislature in Micro-

nesia," 7, *Asian Survey* (1967), 462, 467.

11. Many of the fine photographs in David S. Boyer's "Micronesia: the Americanization of Eden," 132, *National Geographic Magazine* (May 1967), 702–744, are of life in the Yap Islands District.

12. Tadao Yanaihara, *Pacific Islands under Japanese Mandate* (New York: Oxford University Press, 1940), 30.

13. David M. Schneider, "Abortion and Depopulation on a Pacific Island," in Andrew M. Vayda (ed.), *Peoples and Cultures of the Pacific* (Garden City Press, 1963), 383–406.

14. Cf. William A. Lessa, "The Place of Ulithi in the Yap Empire," 9, *Human Organization* (1950), 16.

15. There is a three-tier court system in Micronesia: the High Court, staffed by American judges, and district and community courts, staffed by Micronesians. Trial by jury is used only in the Marianas. Local customary law, particularly in matters relating to land, is applied as well as local legislation and American common law.

CHAPTER 12

Micronesia: The Problem of Status

You can never plan the future by the past.
(Edmund Burke)

I

For Micronesia 1968 was a year of lopsided achievement. The number of Peace Corps volunteers rose to seven-hundred, a high proportion of them involved in teaching English and promoting community development. On the whole the Micronesians were very pleased to have them. Jet airline services, linking Saipan and Guam with Truk and Majuro, swept into the Territory. Before long the aircraft would carry parties of Japanese and American tourists from district to district. High school enrollments were bounding forward; and more than three-hundred Micronesian students were going on to further education outside the Territory. But the base of the economy remained weak. The splendid development plans for district centers had yet to get off the ground. This was hardly surprising, inasmuch as the United States Congress had not in fact appropriated more than twenty million dollars for annual grants to the Territory till fiscal year 1968; and the cost of making good the years of neglect in these remote and scattered islands would be enormous. However, a higher annual ceiling was promised for fiscal years 1970 and 1971. If sums approaching fifty million dollars were indeed to be appropriated and spent on worthwhile projects, this would mark a great leap forward.

The year 1968 was also marked by ostensibly modest constitutional changes. One of these changes, the exclusion of government employees from membership of the Congress of Micronesia, made little difference in practice; but the fact that so many Congressmen were willing to surrender well-paid government jobs in order to remain in politics on a low salary suggests clearly enough that Congress had come to stay. More significant, perhaps, was another feature of the Fourth Amendment to the Secretarial Order. The salaries of Micronesian Congressmen were in future to be paid out of funds appropriated by the United States Congress itself.[1] Obviously this gesture was not intended merely to make more funds available for appropriation by the Congress of Micronesia. It indicated the direction in which thoughts were turning in Washington. Micronesian Congressmen accepted this change without enthusiasm. But then, many of them had drawn salaries as employees of the Territorial Government before this without being reduced to docility.

II

1968 also saw the first fruits of serious local thinking about Micronesian ultimate political status. The story goes back to August 1966, when the Congress of Micronesia petitioned the President of the United States "to establish a commission to consult the people of Micronesia to ascertain their wishes and views, and to study and critically assess the political alternatives open to Micronesia." In 1967 the Congress of Micronesia provided for the establishment of its own Future Political Status Commission. About the same time, the President submitted to the United States Congress a proposal to set up a commission to examine the issues with a view to enabling "the people of the Trust Territory freely to express their wishes as soon as possible, and not later than June 30, 1972, on the future status of the Trust Territory." The President's Status Commission would consist of a chairman and eight members appointed by the President, four members chosen by the President of the Senate, and four chosen by the Speaker of the House of Representatives; it would be required to submit its report and recommendations within eight months of the provision of appropriations.[2] Minor disagreements arose in Congress over the Commission's composition and the target date. The joint resolution failed to pass in 1967, again in the election year of 1968, and yet again in 1969. But in January 1968 members of the Subcommittees on Territorial and Insular Affairs of both the House of Representatives and the Senate visited Micronesia and held discussions with the Micronesian Future Political Status Commission.

These discussions were not published. It is understood, however, that the Micronesians found the American senators more flexible than the members of the House subcommittee. The prevailing view on the House subcommittee is said to have been that independence and statehood were equally unrealistic goals for Micronesia, that its best course would be to elect to become an unincorporated territory of the United States like Guam. In the meantime Micronesia could not expect to be allowed either to appropriate federal grants in aid or to obtain free entry for its products into the United States.

Meanwhile the Future Political Status Commission had not been idle. At its first meeting, in November 1967, it elected as chairman, Representative (now Senator) Lazarus Salii of Palau, the prime mover in this local initiative. It met again in January and April 1968, the meetings lasting some six days each. In May 1968 Representative Salii and Senator Bailey Olter visited the United Nations, Puerto Rico and the United States Virgin Islands in company with a State Department official. At the end of June 1968 the Commission produced its first Interim Report, a document of one-hundred-twenty-five pages.

The Commission, under the terms of the joint resolution authorizing its appointment, consisted of a Congressman from each administrative district. Its terms of reference were (a) to develop and recommend methods of political education, (b) to present the alternative options to Micronesians, (c) to recommend procedures to determine the wishes of the people, (d) "to undertake a comparative analysis and to select areas of study of the manners and procedures whereby the Commonwealth of Puerto Rico, Western Samoa, and Cook Islands, and other territories and developing nations have achieved their self-government, independence, or other status," and (e) to perform any necessary ancillary functions. The mention of "independence" in the terms of reference and also in the preambular recitals to the joint resolution, and the omission of any express reference to American unincorporated territories, were no doubt carefully calculated.

The Interim Report was inconclusive but unusually interesting. The Commission had not yet held public hearings; not yet examined all the issues. It asked the regular session of Congress for renewal of its mandate. This was quickly granted without dissent; Congress appropriated the relatively large sum of seventy thousand dollars for the purpose, to enable the Commission to travel farther afield. Clearly the Interim Report had made a favorable impression.

The Report concentrated on identifying alternative constitutional destinations open to Micronesia. In an appendix it summarized the recent political history of the Commonwealth of Puerto Rico, Western Samoa, the Cook Islands, the Philippines, and Guam, in that order. Analyzing these particular cases, the report pointed out that the territories, upon determination of their present status, had not been economically self-sufficient and that determination of status had not significantly encouraged investment or economic growth. Each of them, neglected by the metropolitan government, looked to local agitation for a change of status and for constitutional reform. In some of them external factors such as United Nations attitudes, or indirect pressure (i.e., the cultivation of influential friends within the metropolitan power structure) had been important. This analysis was cautiously objective, but its gist was not understood to appraise independence as a panacea for Micronesia's ills. However, there was no detailed examination of the circumstances in which an option for independence might be to Micronesia's advantage.

In other appendices, the Commission set out its recommendations for a review of Secretarial Order No. 2882, and its comments on a bill for an Organic Act for the Trust Territory, which Representative Patsy Mink of Hawaii had introduced into the United States Congress. (The bill was not passed into law.) These recommendations and comments probably influenced to some degree the Fourth Amendment to the Secretarial Order, issued three months later. The Commission also concluded that although it should cooperate with the Presidential Status Commission, were it formed, Micronesians should not sit as members of the Presidential Commission.

The Commission recognized the importance of the question of political education, for Micronesians generally lacked adequate understanding of present government institutions and were not in a position to make an informed choice of their future status. Pointless then, to make detailed recommendations on the matter, if only because the Commission itself was still in the process of evaluating the various alternative types of status. But in January 1969 a special committee on Government Organization, to examine ways of improving the efficiency of the Trust Territory Government, was constituted by the Congress of Micronesia. The committee heard testimony from officials and others, and decided to travel to all districts in March. It would be in a position to promote the diffusion of information and perhaps to indicate how best to prepare the people for subsequent self-determination.

The Interim Report gave preliminary consideration to nine possibilities. Three were concerned with the Territory's future geographical limits, six with the ultimate political status of the Territory, assuming retention of existing boundaries; there was some overlap between the several options.

On the question of geographical limits, the courses considered were the expansion of Micronesia to include island areas not yet within its boundaries; the division of Micronesia (perhaps uniting part of the Territory with another political entity); and the maintenance of present Micronesian boundaries.

The expansion of Micronesia to include other areas (e.g., Guam, Nauru, American Samoa, the Cook Islands, the Gilbert and Ellice Islands) presupposed a willingness to unite on the part of the others. Nothing in any of these territories except Guam evidenced any wish to create such a union, nor that union would bring economic advantages. The question of union with Guam would, however, require further investigation.

My own impression was that no body of opinion in Micronesia except that represented by the Popular party in the Marianas—now, for the time being a minority party in its own district—wanted union with Guam. The Popular party wanted the Marianas detached from the rest of Micronesia for this purpose. And in Guam itself opinion seemed more favorable to incorporation of the Marianas than the Trust Territory as a whole. It is of some interest that neither in this context nor elsewhere in the Interim Report was any express reference made to the possibility of union with Hawaii, despite the fact that Governor Burns of Hawaii [3] and other influential figures in that State [4] were known to favor the incorporation of Micronesia within Hawaii. The emphasis in this section of the Interim Report was on the expansion rather than the absorption of Micronesia. By implication, the Commission was unwilling to see Micronesia lose its identity by subordination to another entity.

The Commission felt that, on the whole, division of the Territory offered little. Moreover, fragmentation was opposed both by the United States and by the United Nations. But the decision to proceed on the assumption that the Territory would be preserved as an entity was "a begrudging and tentative conclusion." [5]

The wording reveals differences of opinion within the Commission. This is not surprising. Not only did the Commission include a separatist from the Marianas, but nationalist sentiment in other parts of Micronesia is weak and, as the Commission put it, "embryonic." Were a plebiscite conducted there and then, offering each district the option of separate independence, this option would probably have attracted a very large vote. Local particularism is a potent force in Micronesia. People are more aware of what divides them from their neighbors in other districts than of what unites them. These sentiments are not confined to the apolitical majority. They are shared in some degree by the more sophisticated. Among resolutions passed by the Congress of Micronesia in 1968 was one congratulating the Republic of Nauru on the attainment of independence. A number of prominent Micronesians from various districts hanker after the same goal. But they are practical enough to be pessimistic especially as such miniscule and impoverished entities could hardly maintain a viable independence without offering strategic facilities to a foreign country hostile to the United States. One has only to state the problem to see that it would be almost impossible to resolve. Moreover, if each district decided to go its own way, and the United States and the United Nations were to concur, it is quite certain that some of the new microstates would be left to moulder in stagnation. And if strategic potential is to be used as a bargaining counter in negotiations about ultimate status, there is (quite apart from the attitude of the Administering Authority) a sufficient number of Micronesians with an interest in maintaining the Territory's geographical integrity to quash any serious separatist agitation at present. If a district has a valuable asset, pressure will be for an auction on behalf of the people of the whole Territory.

On the provisional assumption that the Territory would remain one, the Commission set out four alternative destinations: independence; the status of a freely associated state or protectorate; integration with a sovereign state; and (perhaps surprisingly) continuance as a trust territory. The Commission made comments on these several possibilities but offered no recommendations.

The Commission briefly stated the implications of independence, but in so delicate a manner as to give no direct offense to the Administering Authority. It went on to observe that lack of money and manpower, and general economic underdevelopment, presented serious obstacles to independence in the near future, unless one form of economic and political dependence were exchanged for another. The Commission concluded with the cryptic observation that "in considering an independent Micronesia . . . some thought must be given to the continuing strategic interest of the United States in Micronesia." [6] One could assume that these words were not composed in a spirit of altruism. Micronesians would not voluntarily eschew independence merely in order to safeguard the interests of the United States. The passage implied that American presence in Micronesia might well be worth a great deal of money to the United States, especially if the Ryuku Islands (including Okinawa) were to be evacuated soon; it implied, too, that an option for independence would not inevitably prove an economic catastrophe, despite the serious risks (i.e., the unpopularity of foreign aid in the United States Congress, and the unpredictability of strategic appreciations); and that nobody could be sure of American reactions to a vote in favor of independence. One can at least be sure—and the Micronesians are aware of this—that the United States Government would prefer Micronesia *not* to opt for independence; and that it can be persuaded to invest a good deal of money in developing Micronesian resources in the hope of influencing the outcome.

The Commission dwelt even less expansively on the status of what it called a "free associated state," which it equated with a protectorate. It had not studied, at that time, arrangements for the British associated states in the Caribbean. One of the appendices described rather sketchily the constitutional and economic position in the Cook Islands.

The next group of possible destinations were forms of integration with a major power. "The logical choice for integration," in the words of the Report, "is with the United States." Such a choice would practically guarantee continued support for development programs and for the supply of skilled personnel not available in Micronesia. Three forms of "integration" were mentioned: Commonwealth status after the style of Puerto Rico; integration as an unincorporated territory; and integration as an incorporated territory. The Report did not deal with the possibility of separate statehood for Micronesia, except in passing when it referred to the status of an incorporated territory as the "highest next to statehood" within the American system. Nor, as we have pointed out, did it mention the question of union with Hawaii.

The present writer's own impression is that most of the members of the Commission were attracted to the idea of Commonwealth status but not to territorial status. They did not wish to be latter-day Guamanians or appendages of Hawaii; nor, for that matter, did they appear to be enamored of the concept of American citizenship or liability to the draft, which the Puerto Ricans enjoy. But Puerto Rico's wide measure of internal autonomy coupled with a de facto right of self-determination, viewed against a background of impressive economic development and participation in a range of American social welfare programs, had much to commend it. Why the Commission distinguished Commonwealth status so sharply from free association according to the Cook Islands model was not clear. The Cook Islanders have retained New Zealand citizenship and free access to New Zealand. The economy is heavily subsidized by New Zealand. And the Islands have an explicit constitutional right to opt for independence. It is true that the Cook Islands do not enjoy high living standards, and they do not share fully in the social benefits of New Zealand. But then the islands are very remote and poor in resources, and New Zealand is a fairly small and not particularly rich country. Moreover, it is open to the Cook Islands Legislature to enact measures for reasonable protective discrimination in favor of the indigenous inhabitants.

Finally, there was the possibility of remaining a trust territory indefinitely. Such a decision might expedite the economic development by leaving the United States exposed to pressure; if the status issue were resolved, there was a danger that Micronesia would be allowed to fall back into oblivion.

This last suggestion would be unattractive to the United States Government, to international opinion and to a growing number of educated Micronesians.[7] If such a state of affairs were to come to pass it would be a by-product either of disagreement with the United States or within Micronesia on the status issue, or of failure to persuade the United Nations that the trusteeship agreement should be terminated—for example, because the Micronesians had opted for a status less than sovereign independence.

III

In July 1969 the Micronesian Future Political Status Commission issued its final Report. It came down in favor of an internally self-governing state in free association with the United States. If negotiations for free association were to fail, the Commission recommended that Micronesia ultimately opt for independence as a unified state.[8]

During the preceding few months there had been several developments. First, the Commission had engaged Professor James W. Davidson of the Australian National University, Canberra, as its constitutional consultant. Davidson, a New Zealander, was entirely independent of the Territorial Administration. He had been one of the architects of the Cook Islands free association scheme and Western Samoa's independence constitution. In 1967 he had advised Hammer De Roburt in Nauru during the difficult but successful negotiations for independence. His appointment to advise the Micronesian Commission was an astute and significant move.

Second, the Congress of Micronesia had become a body of salaried members, and the length of its usual sessions for 1969 had been doubled. The fact that salaries were paid out of American congressional appropriations underlined the difficulties implicit in an option for independence. But the status of Micronesian congressmen had been enhanced rather than diminished in their own eyes and the eyes of the electorate. And as professional legislators, excluded from both executive power and effective participation in decision-making, they became more, not less, self-assertive.

Third, the Status Commission had broadened its horizons by talking to the political leaders of Nauru and the Cook Islands, and visiting American Samoa, Western Samoa, Fiji, and Australian New Guinea.

Fourth, it conducted public hearings in each of the six districts in order to sound local opinion and further political education.

Fifth, the election results in the Marianas had reduced the dimensions of the problem created by the separatist movement in that district.

Sixth, in April 1969 the Commission issued a Statement of Intent, virtually a synopsis of the conclusions contained in its Report three months later.

Seventh, in May 1969 the new Secretary of the Interior, the new Director of the Office of Territories,[9] and high-ranking defense officials visited Micronesia. The ball was already in their court, and they were in a position to assess the nature of America's problems.

Eighth, it was becoming increasingly likely that the United States would (1) relinquish its political status in Okinawa, where it had massive bases, and (2) phase out its commitment in Vietnam, during the next few years. The net result would probably be an increase in the strategic "denial" value of Micronesia to the United States. But it was impossible to predict how the change of Government in Washington and the introduction of new faces among those responsible for the Territory's affairs [10] would affect the Administration's policies.

Other changes, not so immediately relevant, were taking place in Micronesia. The growth in tourism [11] was beginning to make a real impact. A new communications system linked all six districts. An airstrip was being completed in Ponape. And commercial television for Saipan was envisioned for the end of 1969.

At a more mundane level, agriculture, fisheries and public works still languished. But there was an improvement in interisland surface vessel communications. Bikini was being rehabilitated. Peace Corps personnel were being reduced from seven hundred to four hundred following an evaluation of its own performance by the Peace Corps, and the vast majority were to be engaged in training Micronesian teachers in English teaching. The Territorial Government decided to shift the emphasis in education from concentration on liberal arts courses towards a vocational approach. And in April 1969 the United States had at last persuaded the Japanese Government to come to an agreement over the long-standing Micronesian grievances about war damage claims. Each government agreed to contribute five million dollars in settlement of the claims, the United States paying the sum in cash and the Japanese in kind. Ten million dollars might be a paltry recompense for the suffering endured twenty-five years ago, but it was not a derisory amount.

IV

The 1969 Report of the Future Status Commission was far more decisive and explicit than the Interim Report. It summarily dismissed integration with Japan as being neither advantageous nor practicable. It rejected the idea of integration with the United States,[12] while recognizing the economic benefits that incorporation with the American constitutional system would bring. The disadvantages, paramount in the eyes of the Commission, were five: other United States citizens would have equal rights to acquire land[13] and conduct business in Micronesia; Micronesia would lack control of its own affairs; Micronesians would be subject to United States taxes; they would have fewer opportunities to hold key positions in the government; there would be intensified Americanization, which would diminish the prospect of preserving Micronesian cultures. The Report failed to make it clear, however, that some of these consequences would flow only from complete integration—e.g., as part of the State of Hawaii. Guam, an unincorporated territory of the United States, has a large measure of internal self-government; Guamanians hold most of the key positions in the Administration; the tax system is not the same as on the mainland. But to the Micronesians (except in the Marianas) America is no more than a generous and helpful friend. Most Micronesians, unlike Guamanians, do not *want* to be incorporated into the great American family; they do not feel that they are or ought to be Americans. Nor do they wish to have their hands tied by the Pentagon. Their aversion from territorial status rests to a large extent on a distaste for the situation in Guam, which they see as inimical to self-respect. To the members of the Status Commission, a merger with Guam imposed by the United States while Micronesia was still a trust territory would be unacceptable.

Nevertheless, the Commission took note of sentiment in the Marianas District in favor of an immediate merger with Guam, and of the interest shown at its public hearings in all districts in relationships with Guam. It dealt judiciously with the separatist movement on the Marianas, and went so far as to declare that it "would not oppose a political union which reflects the freely-expressed desire of a majority of the residents of the district."[14] But it also commented that it was ultimately for the United States and the United Nations to resolve this question, and expressed the hope that separation would not be embarked upon till all possibilities for partnership had been explored.

The Commission foresaw a growth in cooperation between Guam and the Trust Territory, and thought it "not impossible" that Guam and Micronesia might one day comprise a single political unit.[15] But first the Trust Territory had to become a self-governing state in free association with the United States. If the people of Guam were to join the people of the Trust Territory in a movement towards full internal self-government, the question of a future union could be carefully discussed.[16] This part of the Commission's Report was cautiously and somewhat vaguely worded, perhaps for the purpose of securing unanimity on a contentious issue. Union between a self-governing Micronesia and Guam may indeed not be "impossible"; but there would have to be big changes of attitude in both territories before it could be seriously contemplated.

On the central issues, the Commission shed the reticence it had shown in 1968. Micronesia had to become fully self-governing "because the continuation of a quasi-colonial status would prove degrading to Micronesia and unworthy of America."[17] But America had strategic interests in the area. For this purpose it needed to use the Micronesians' most precious asset, their land; and it should be prepared to pay an appropriate price, freely negotiated with Micronesians, for such facilities. The price would entail the provision of material and human aid to the Micronesian Government, and the representation and protection of Micronesia in international affairs. In return, Micronesia would accept some relinquishment of land for American military purposes, the social consequences of the presence of American military personnel, and the prospect of being a target in a future war.

The Commission envisaged the following procedure. First, a formal request by the Congress of Micronesia to the United States Congress for the passage of an enabling Act similar to the Act under which Puerto Rico's Commonwealth (or free association) constitution was adopted by the people; second, negotiations by Micronesian representatives with the Federal Government in Washington;[18] third, the adoption of an extensive program of political education in Micronesia, inspired by the initiative of individual members of the Congress of Micronesia; fourth, the election of a Constitutional Convention in Micronesia to determine the future constitution; fifth, submission of both the constitution prepared by the Convention and the question of political status accompanying it to a referendum of the people. If the proposals were rejected by the people, trusteeship would have to be prolonged till a satisfactory solution was reached. If the proposals were rejected by the voters of a single district, the Congress of Micronesia "should take this into careful consideration and attempt to resolve it." [19] The Commission was clear that the constitution could not be one handed down by the Administering Authority, and that close consultation with the United Nations should be maintained.

The Commission did not offer detailed suggestions for the future structure of internal self-government, but noted a consensus that the interests of each district ought to be taken into account; that no district or group of districts be allowed a dominating position by reason of numerical superiority; and that unity must be compatible with decentralization and the recognition of diversity. It might be desirable to vest executive power in a council representing all districts instead of concentrating that power in one individual.

Perhaps the best section of the Report was the succinct appraisal of the advantages and disadvantages of independence.[20] An independent Micronesia would need to have close ties with a major power, presumably the United States, and would depend on that power for grants in aid and rental for leased strategic bases. An attempt by that power to exert undue pressure on an independent Micronesia would be more difficult than if Micronesia were its associated state. Its authority in an independent Micronesia would be defined by treaty. As an independent state Micronesia could, if it wished, take part directly in the affairs of international organizations; it would have more freedom of maneuver. The Commission also thought that a decision to opt for independence would assist the growth of national pride and a sense of Micronesian identity. Independence, moreover, would be an outcome acceptable to the United Nations.

On the other hand, the absence of a formal constitutional link with the United States would leave Micronesia in a perilous economic position as one among many claimants for foreign aid. Even if the American Government felt a sense of obligation, their sympathy might not be shared by Congress. As an independent state, Micronesia could not expect duty-free entry for its exports to the United

States or so ready a supply of American expert advisers, though it would be free to seek assistance elsewhere. However, independence would probably mean a fall in Micronesia's already low living standards. Given the "grim realities" of Micronesian conditions, the Commission recommended independence "only as a second alternative to be considered if self-government in free association with the United States should not be possible." Earlier in the Report the Commission had stressed that failure in the negotiations with the United States should not lead to "an abrupt and immediate plunge into the hardships and uncertainties of independence" but to a lengthy prolongation of the Trusteeship Agreement while the basis for viable Micronesian independence was being established.[21]

In two respects the Commission seems to have been unrealistic. First independence would be more likely to lead to insular fragmentation than to national unity, except possibly in the very short term. One clear advantage of association with the United States would be that America could be expected to apply coercion to a secessionist island group. It might be more reluctant to do so at the invitation of an independent Micronesian Government. Second, it is hard to believe that the United Nations would recognize the validity of an act of self-determination which did not offer the Micronesians the *option* of voting for independence.

The Report is markedly vague on the type of association arrangement the Commission had in mind. From its omissions one may perhaps infer that the Commission favored a relationship with the United States less close than that of Puerto Rico but not quite as loose as that between New Zealand and the Cook Islands. Nothing in the Report suggests that the association arrangements should include a provision (which exists in the Cook Islands and the British associated states) for termination at the instance of either party. Presumably this omission reflects the fear that Micronesia might one day be cast adrift to fend for itself. But the independence option cannot be dismissed so easily. Again, the Report seems to assume that Micronesians (unlike Puerto Ricans) would not be American citizens, but should enjoy free access to the United States and the American market, whereas American citizens would not enjoy corresponding rights of access to Micronesia; and that the United States Government and Congress would lack paramount authority in Micronesia (as New Zealand lacks paramount authority in the Cook Islands) except in relation to external defense and international relations. However, it is understandable that the Micronesians should seek the best of all available worlds. It is also understandable that, whatever the Report may say, continued association with the United States would be, for many Micronesians, a second best, a sacrifice of their emotional preference for independence.

V

America's self-image has been and still is that of a noncolonial, indeed anticolonial, power. For a number of reasons this image is no longer credible in much of the inaptly named "third world." [22] American interests have demanded support for a western alliance with colonial powers; military intervention in small countries menaced or thought to be menaced by Communist subversion or takeovers; the maintenance of foreign bases; and the adoption of positions in the Middle East and Southern Africa too moderate to satisfy inflamed passions. In addition, the United States remains subject to the hostile scrutiny of the Committee of Twenty-Four because of its "colonial" stance in Guam, the Virgin Islands, American Samoa and Micronesia. It has the disadvantage of being wealthy in a world of poor nations; it is accused of neo-colonialism. It houses the United Nations in New York, where delegates can observe for themselves a wide gulf between riches and squalor, surges of black revolutionary sentiment, and violent manifestations of social disorder.

The international image of the United States may improve; it may deteriorate. In any event, the influence wielded by the United States at the United Nations and in the world at large is more impressive than America's popularity. Its success (for what it is worth) in securing the exclusion of Communist China from the Chinese seat at the United Nations for so many years bears testimony to this fact. But in such a context the United States must surely handle the problem of Micronesia with delicacy and finesse, unless, of course, it is prepared to thumb its nose at United Nations opinion in defense of an interest inessential to national survival.

Relations between the United States and the Trusteeship Council have been amicable. The comments of the 1967 Visiting Mission to Micronesia were far from being uniformly uncomplimentary. At the conclusion of the debate on Micronesia in the Trusteeship Council in June 1968 the senior American representative, a newcomer to these proceedings, was moved to observe that he had "never met a group of members of any [United Nations] body who could surpass, or even match in courtesy, co-operation and diligence, the members of this Council." [23] The Trusteeship Council is now a waning force. Its proceedings attract little attention. At the Council's second meeting on Micronesia in May 1968 none of the sixty-six seats in the press gallery was occupied. Attendance in the public gallery—admittedly on a wet morning—varied from one to four. One spectator fell asleep. However, the Trusteeship Council, provided that it survives, may play an important role in the process of self-determination for Micronesia, if only because among the organs of the United Nations it is the least unsympathetic to American viewpoints and by far the best informed about the problems of the area. A Visiting Mission from the Trusteeship Council is going to Micronesia early in 1970. It may well be the last. America's interests dictate that the Visiting Mission's Report be generally favorable. That Report is unlikely to be favorable to the Administering Authority unless there are clear signs that (1) preparations for an act of self-determination are on their way and (2) Micronesians will be left to choose their own ultimate status and not have that status thrust upon them.

It does not follow that America must totally endorse the recommendations of the Micronesian Future Political Status Commission or offer a blank cheque to Micronesia.

Given the general climate of opinion in the United Nations, it is essential (1) that Micronesia be offered a genuine independence option and (2) that the conduct of a referendum on the staus issue be supervised or observed by United Nations representatives. There is no precedent for a trust territory opting for a status other than independence in its own right or as part of a contiguous independent state. If Micronesia is not going to opt for independence, moderate anti-colonial opinion at the United Nations must at least be satisfied that the Micronesians really do not want independence. This cannot be demonstrated unless the Micronesians are offered the option, even if they would prefer not to be offered it. And the offer (which could be postdated) should not be accompanied by threats of cessation of all economic aid if the Micronesians were to vote for independence; otherwise the people's choice of an association arrangement might be justly criticized as having been made under duress. It must be borne in mind too that, since the Anguillan episode, free association is widely regarded as colonialism masquerading under a thin disguise.

Termination of the Trusteeship Agreement must be approved not only by the United States Government (see Agreement, Art. 15) and Congress but also by the Security Council. The General Assembly has no *locus standi,* since Micronesia is a strategic trust territory. If the Administering Authority purported to terminate the Agreement unilaterally, this would be ineffective in international law.[24] The United Nations Charter is strangely silent on the procedure to be adopted; but we can assume that (1) any resolution to terminate the Agreement must be passed by the Security Council and (2) each permanent member of the Security Council would have a right of veto. In addition, the matter would probably be construed as sufficiently important to require an affirmative vote of nine of the fifteen members of the Security Council, including the concurring votes of the permanent members.[25] The onus of satisfying an anti-colonial majority of the Security Council will not easily be discharged. Perhaps the United States will be able to come to an understanding with the Soviet Union. If, however, Peking has occupied the Chinese seat by the time the issue comes before the Security Council, the prospects of a veto will be very real. For this reason alone the United States will be well advised to treat the question of ultimate status as urgent. If, moreover, things go wrong at the United Nations, if a referendum cannot be conducted with the blessing of the United Nations, or if its outcome is unacceptable to the Security Council, the United States will remain saddled with a trust territory for which it is no longer prepared to be internationally accountable. This state of affairs, leaving the United States barraged by international criticism and harried by ungrateful wards, ought to be avoided if possible.

The United States should therefore be accommodating to the Micronesians. It should, however, make it clear that any association arrangement submitted to the people for approval must include provision for unilateral termination of the arrangement, enabling the Micronesians subsequently to proceed to independence if they so wished. Preferably that option for unilateral termination should extend to the Micronesians alone. But it would be asking a good deal of the United States not to insist on a reciprocal right to terminate the association.

The Micronesians ought not to be offered the choice of fragmentation. There is no dearth of particularist sentiment, and to legitimize it would be to encourage it, to the detriment of the Territory as a whole. To afford the Marianas the option of seceding to join Guam would be very badly received at the United Nations. Possibly the least unsatisfactory solution to this problem would be for the Constitution of Micronesia to provide that within a prescribed period *after* Micronesia had attained associated status (or independence) a referendum be held on the issue in the Marianas District.

From all this it follows that the United States should be prepared to risk its own interests in Micronesia in order not to thwart Micronesia's desire for autonomy and thereby antagonize the great bulk of international opinion. Temptation to palm Micronesia off with territorial status, either as a new unincorporated territory or as part of Guam, must be firmly resisted. Micronesians outside the Marianas do not want such a status. There is no precedent for the annexation of a trust territory by an Administering Authority; and the status of an unincorporated territory is regarded by the United Nations as more "colonial" than that of a trust territory. True, America's defense interests could be better protected by the incorporation of Micronesia than by any other constitutional arrangement. The embarrassment of seeing "immature" Micronesia leapfrog the Virgin Islands, Guam and American Samoa by achieving full internal self-government in a sudden bound would also be avoided. Again, there is a lot of ocean within the boundaries of Micronesia, which might yield wealth to be exploited one day. And the economic future of the Micronesians would become less uncertain. But the international image of the United States would be gravely damaged by such an imposition.

The general guide-lines for the United States to follow have been indicated by the Report of the Future Status Commission. An outsider would be presumptuous to prescribe the manner in which a scheme for association should be negotiated. Clearly United States congressional leaders must be brought into the picture at an early stage; enabling legislation will be required, and it must not be allowed to suffer the fate of the Joint Resolutions on the Presidential Status Commission [26] or the dismal delays in implementing proposals for constitutional change in the Virgin Islands.

Meanwhile, development aid to Micronesia must somehow produce tangible results. This will at least help to dispel the pervasive sense of pessimism in Micronesia. Rome cannot, and yet it must, be built in a day and a half; and it must be built in the hearts and minds of Micronesians. Above all, Micronesians who are in politics must feel that they have a meaningful voice in shaping their country's destiny. Leading members of the Congress of Micronesia must be brought into closer association with the Territorial Government, participating directly in the formation and implementation of local policy decisions.

Their views on the question of Micronesia's future status—views which, by modern international standards, are distinctly moderate—must be listened to with the greatest respect in Washington. And within an agreed framework, the elected representatives of the Micronesians must then be allowed to evolve, in a Constitutional Convention, their own form of government, free from external constraint. If these principles are applied without procrastination, there is every possibility that the people of Micronesia will determine their future by opting for free association with the United States.

NOTES

1. Travel and subsistence allowances were to be met out of local funds appropriated by the Congress of Micronesia. At the same time, the salary of the Legislative Counsel to the Congress became payable out of the funds appropriated by the Congress of Micronesia instead of the High Commissioner's budget.

2. See *Congressional Record:* Senate, §12111–12113 (August 23, 1967).

3. The Governor's views are reported in the *Guam Daily News,* July 5, 1968, p. 4.

4. See *Reports on Pacific Affairs 1965:* Hearings before the Subcommittee on Territorial and Insular Affairs of the Committee on Interior and Insular Affairs, House of Representatives, 89th Congress, 1st Session (August 5 and 11, and September 7, 1965) (Serial No. 16–54–164, Washington, D.C.).

5. Interim Report, p. 17.

6. Interim Report, p. 21.

7. Though many persons to whom the members of the Trusteeship Council's Visiting Mission of 1967 spoke had asked them: "Why is the United Nations rushing us? What is the hurry?" (Report, T/1658, S 317.)

8. In July 1968 I had intimated to certain members of the Commission that if I had been asked to advise them, my own provisional inclination would have been to advise them broadly along such lines. I have no reason to suppose, however, that this informal and tentative expression

of opinion carried any real weight.

9. Mrs. Elizabeth P. Farrington, replacing Mrs. Ruth G. Van Cleve after the inauguration of the Nixon administration.

10. High Commissioner William R. Norwood, a conscientious and respected public servant, was replaced in 1969 by Edward E. Johnston, a businessman and chairman of the Hawaii State Republican Party. Initial reactions in Micronesia were cool. Peter Coleman, the well-liked district administrator for the Marianas, and former Governor of American Samoa —he is a part-Samoan—was appointed to the new post of Deputy High Commissioner for the Territory.

11. For fiscal year 1969 there was an increase of 40% to twelve thousand.

12. Report, 48–49.

13. The possibility of an American Samoan solution was not considered in the Report, perhaps because the constitutionality of protective discrimination in favor of the Samoans was questionable.

14. Report, 37.

15. *Ibid.,* 38.

16. *Ibid.,* 39–40.

17. *Ibid.,* 8. (Statement of Intent)

18. Preliminary discussions were taking place in the fall of 1969.

19. Report, 43.

20. Report, 45–48.

21. *Ibid.,* 25.

22. See, on these matters, two penetrating articles by Kenneth Twitchett, "The American National Interest and the Anti-Colonial Crusade," 3, *International Relations* (London: David Davies Memorial Institute of International Studies, 1967), 273–295; "The United States and *le Tiers Monde,*" *ibid.* (1968), 328–354.

23. United Nations Document T/PV.1341 (June 19, 1968), 62.

24. See *Advisory Opinion on the International Status of Southwest Africa* (1950), I.C.J. Reports 128.

25. See Charter, Article 27(3) as amended; Geoffrey Marston, "Termination of Trusteeship," 18, *International and Comparative Law Quarterly,* 1–40 (1969), 13.

26. Three days after the presentation of the Future Political Status Commission's Report, the Congress of Micronesia adopted a Joint Resolution "urgently requesting the President and Congress of the United States to give serious consideration to the future political status of Micronesia and the ways in which this status should be finally resolved. . . ." This Joint Resolution was laid before the United States Congress as a petition. See *Congressional Record—Senate,* §8641 (July 28, 1969).

Index